The Door to Heaven is Open,

Come on In

Beth Reeves

ISBN 978-1-64258-068-6 (paperback)
ISBN 978-1-64258-069-3 (digital)

Christian Faith Publishing, Inc.
832 Park Avenue
Meadville, PA 16335
www.christianfaithpublishing.com

Printed in the United States of America

To my dear, sweet, Heavenly Father
and His precious Son, my friend, Jesus.

The Lord Comes

Now learn a parable of the fig tree; when his branch is yet tender,
and putteth forth leaves, yea, know that summer is nigh:

So likewise ye, when ye shall see all these things,
know that it is near, even at the doors.

Watch therefore: for ye know not what hour your Lord doth come:

Therefore be ye also ready: for in such an hour as ye think not,
the Son of Man cometh!
—Matthew 24: 32–33, 42, and 44 (KJV)

Because Jesus is not only the source of abundant life,
but Jesus, being made perfect, He became the author
of eternal salvation unto all them that obey Him.

—Hebrews 5:9

I obeyed you Jesus, and here is your book!
Thank you for allowing me to be a vessel of
your Holy Word! I love you, dear Jesus!

—Beth Reeves

The Door to Heaven Is Open: Come on In!

The door to heaven is open; come on in! Come on in!
Now is the time; if you're to be saved from sin!
Enter, enter all, don't you hear my call?
I'm calling, calling you home;
The door to heaven is open, come on in!
Come home, come on home;
Give me your all, I'm calling you now! The door
to heaven is still open; come on in!
I hear your hearts bleeding,
I hear what you are needing.
I am your Lord!
Hear my call!
My door to heaven is still open;
Come on home!
Come on home!

—Beth Reeves

"Praise God! Praise God!" I can now finally say those words, out loud, at last! I have carried these words around in my heart, for the last forty-one years, but I have not had the courage to say them out loud! Thank you, Jesus, for giving me that courage now! I want to yell it from the rooftops or go climb a mountain, stretch out my arms, and yell, "Praise You, Lord!" from the top of my lungs! I'm getting ahead of my story, forgive me, but when you believe in Jesus, you do tend to get excited.

And it seems impossible to keep quiet.

Jesus has wanted me to sit down and write of my experiences with him, for years. I have always felt like many persons before me that I could not write anything—at least not anything that anyone would be interested in reading.

But praise God, here I am sitting quietly and letting God guide my hand and writing the words he wishes me to write. You are going to read these words, all throughout this book, God wants me to tell all of you.

So for the Glory of my dear Lord, I write this book. My prayers are for all of mankind. Please, heed the call of God. He is calling each and every one of you, now. We need to turn our hearts toward home.

God has spoken to me throughout my whole life. But 90 percent of that time, before, about two years ago, I smothered His beautiful, small, still voice. God forgive me, but that is what I did. The good Lord has always been with me. And that is not to say that there hasn't been lots of ups and downs in my life, because I have had my share of sorrow and heartache. But because of God and who He is and the obstacles in my life, God has made me a stronger person.

We can be strong if we lean on the Lord and above all believe in Christ!

My grandmother Rossman was a beautiful person. I would sit at her knee and listen to her talk about God and her relationship with Him. She would tell me about the beautiful angel that always visited her whenever she was troubled or someone else needed prayer or help.

She taught me about the love of Jesus and how wonderful He is in your life! After all these years, her angel stories are still in my mind. It always comforted me to know that we each have an angel of mercy to watch over us. My grandmother Rossman was one of the sweetest ladies you could ever wish to know. I bet she looks very, very beautiful with her angel wings in heaven. She has visited me several times in my dreams since she died. She would hold out her arms toward me in each dream and I would be enveloped in her arms. She would hold me and tell me everything was going to be all right and that she loved me.

In one dream, she was in a huge hall-like room and was dressed in the most beautiful white dress with gold shimmering all throughout the entire dress. She glowed so brightly! She was so beautiful, so beautiful. It is hard to describe the joy in looking at her face! Sometimes it seems almost impossible to describe how exquisitely beautiful things are when the Lord is showing you His ways. How utterly glorious Jesus is when you experience Him in your life!

I truly believe that God visits some people in their dreams. He has given me glimpses of such splendor. I am so thankful that God was there all the time, waiting patiently for me to come to him.

I remember all my life having this one particular dream where I could see God's son, Jesus, coming down from the sky, from the beautiful clouds, coming for all of us. Oh, what a glorious, glorious feeling seeing our dear sweet Jesus coming, drifting slowly downward with His arms outstretched wide coming for all mankind.

Even now it is still an incredible feeling to relive those dreams. When we open our hearts to Jesus, oh how very wonderful life can be for us! As I said before, only on occasion did I listen to that beautiful still voice inside me; about two years ago, I almost died, just from a simple toothache. While I was on the operating table, I had just been told I would probably die and that I needed to prepare my soul. I prayed to my heavenly Father like I had never prayed before in my entire life.

I prayed, "Dear Lord, please let me live. I have not done the things you have wanted me to do all these years. I vow, I promise, I will live my life completely for you for the rest of my life! Please let me live. I will make it up to you for all the times I let you down. And Lord, I am going to be a grandmother one day. I want to see my family grow and happy and to grow old with my beloved husband, Bob. Lord, I love you. Let me live for you!"

Thank the Lord, He heard my prayer, and I lived!

It was hard for the next six to eight months. I tried harder than I had ever tried to obey the Lord's voice when He told me to do something. But I was still trying to live my life my way. Sometimes I obeyed, but not every day as I should have. I have always been a quiet person. I was afraid to speak up or give an opinion about any subject, even my faith. I felt so deeply about Christ our Savior, but there was no way I could get up in front of anyone and say anything. I was just like so many others who are afraid they will look foolish or silly. I never wanted anyone to see me break down and cry or see me just praise the Lord—out loud. Aren't we foolish? As if hearing someone say "praise the Lord" in a soft or loud voice could be foolish. It is so beautiful to hear those words spoken. Because it really doesn't matter what others see or what they think. The only factor is your relationship with God and His Son, Jesus!

I believe in miracles, and I've seen a soul I set free, miraculous the change in one redeemed through Calvary. I believe in miracles, for I believe in God! These words are certainly true for me and for any beautiful soul that has been set free. Praise God!

And even though I am the voice of one crying in the wilderness, I say, "Make straight the way of the Lord!" And I shall talk of the Lord's wondrous works. It feels so wonderful to worship with the people of a church, but what is most important is our relationship with the Lord—a one-on-one relationship with our God. And when God comes for us, His children, it will be because of our faith in Him, not for our faith in our church or our loved ones. That does not mean the church and our loved ones are not important because they most certainly are! But it is our relationship with God alone that is of utmost importance, each and every person, one-on-one with Him.

God had spoken to me all my life, and He nudged me to do His work. But sadly I have hid my light and pushed His voice away by saying, "God, I will do this thing you want me to do—tomorrow," or something like, "I can't be doing this thing, because I will look stupid!" Thank God he forgives us for our sins; He doesn't give up on us.

I hear the words "that God is dead, and no one cares about anyone else anymore." Well, I'm here to tell you, "God is alive!" He cares about us very much. It's just that the old devil is always in there, ready to slap us back down and cause us grief and sorrow. We just have to keep believing in God, no matter what happens.

I feel so much sorrow for those persons who cannot put all their belief in Him. So let's—each and every one of us strong believers—share a little of our faith and belief with one of those who need a little extra belief.

I have a beautiful spiritual friend (that's what I call her). She's very beautiful and her name is Ellen. One night I was visiting her at her house and she read me the most beautiful prayer that she had written, and I want to share it with all of you.

> Do not forget me, oh Lord. Make me strong, as I am weak. Make me the person you want. Keep my enemies away from me. You are so good to me; but as a weak vessel, I need your constant help, in the world and spiritually. Heap

upon me all your blessings to preserve me in the world and from the enemies' harm. I ask this in Jesus's name. Amen.

Isn't that beautiful? Ellen and her family lived next door to us for two years. Was it ever a blessing to know her and her husband Don and their two children, Travis and Terra! God worked through that lovely family to help Bob and me. Ellen taught me or helped me to be able to speak up and be able to reveal my joy in Jesus. Thank you, Jesus for giving me that special friend, Ellen, as my spiritual friend to help me!

Don and Ellen kept inviting Bob and me to go to their church. We finally went one Sunday, and it felt as if we belonged there!

Last November 1987 was "work on and pray for my brother" week. My dear brother Robert is one of God's lost ones that has strayed from God's flock. It was about two days before Thanksgiving. A friend of ours called me and told me my brother needed our help and prayers. I agreed, but I told her it was God's help that he needed and all that we could do was believe in God and pray. Later that evening, I was going to take some things out to my sister-in-law's house way out in the country. I drove a different way (God was leading me and I didn't even know it at the time), and as I came to the intersection and waited for the light to change, I saw that I was across the street from where my brother lived. I had never been to his place; God wanted me to be a witness to Robert and just tell him what had been happening in our lives the last couple of months. As I arrived in the motel room, Robert wasn't there but had left a note on his door stating that he was across the street at the bar.

I told God, "Well, I tried, so I guess I'll just go on out to Sherri's place!"

I started to drive out of the driveway but God told me, "Go the other way!"

So I backed up and said, "Okay, God, I'll go over there, but please have Robert standing on the outside at the phone booth on the corner."

I pulled up to the intersection and looked across the street and there on the corner, talking into the telephone, was Robert!

I shouted, "Thank you, Jesus!"

I went over and asked my brother if he wanted to ride out with me to Sherri's house as we hadn't talked in a long time. God was teaching me, even then, when not to push people. He is such a good God! He knows us, inside and out, and what is best for us if we would all only listen to Him. Anyway, all the way out to Sherri's house (she lives about fifteen miles away from us), I witnessed to Robert and told him all the wonderful changes in my life.

I told him how one night, real late at night, I got down on my knees and this is what I prayed to our dear Lord: "Dear Lord, I am so weary, so tired of this life the way it is now, please come into my heart and change me. Please come into my heart now. I do not like my life or the world as it is today. I believe people are good and that this world can be a better place for all mankind. Lord, please," I sobbed and sobbed, "use me as your vessel and help me to live for you and live as I truly believe!"

And as I said that prayer, a peace came over me that I can't even describe. It was so very beautiful and it made me feel very humble.

Robert didn't say very much. After we got to Sherri's and had visited for a while and left, I asked Robert, "I have heard that you used to travel with Oral Roberts in his gospel group and sing, is this true?"

Robert told me this was true. I told him how wonderful this was and wasn't it strange how after forty-one years of being brother and sister I did not know this about him. We think we know people, but we sometimes don't. He talked all the way home about his days of singing and traveling with Oral Roberts and how much he had loved every minute of it.

When I dropped him off at his motel room, I felt happy and sad for him all at the same time. Here is a man who loved God greatly at one time; what has happened to him? All he cares about now is drinking. We are praying for his soul, and he is going to belong to God again. God loves all His people. We want them to return to Him! Let's all pray that people everywhere will return to accept God's sweet love.

If you are reading this and you don't know Jesus or you've known Him and gone astray, tell God, "Please come into my heart, and change my life. I surrender all to you. I believe in you. I love you."

God will indeed change your life and make you a beautiful new creature. Praise God! Praise God!

A few weeks later, I asked my brother Robert to come to our church. He said he would see. My sister-in-law Sherri saw Robert and she asked him also to come to church. Robert told her also he would see. Sherri and I both felt we weren't to push him. We didn't say anything else about church. But come Sunday that week, our friend Nadine called me three times in one day to ask me to please go and ask Robert to go to church. So by the third time she asked, I figured it was God wanting me to go and ask Robert to come for church in the evening service. So I said, "Okay, I am going to."

We had forty minutes till church started. As I drove down the road in the car, I prayed, "Lord, please let him be in his room or on the other corner of the road this time."

Just as I pulled up to the intersection by Robert's motel, I looked up and there across the street, Robert was standing at the corner, pushing the button of the traffic signal to cross the street.

I shouted, "Thank you, Jesus. Thank you once again." The odds of my brother being on the corner two straight times was so small, that all a person could do was praise God. God had put him on those street corners and the Lord sent me to get Robert. God works in such wonderful ways.

So I pulled over to the side of the road and my brother, Robert, came over to the truck and said, "What are you doing here again?"

I told him God has sent me to get him for church. He gave me three or four excuses why he couldn't go, but for every excuse he gave, God gave me more reasons why He wanted Robert to come to church that particular night! Finally Robert asked me, "Why does God want me to come to church tonight?"

I told him, "Robert, I honestly do not know, I only do as God asks me to do. I don't know what God's reasons are!"

He looked at his watch and said, "I have thirty minutes, then I will come to church."

I thought to myself, *Yes, you have thirty minutes before you go to God's house!* Isn't God wonderful?

So God said, "Let Robert go!" I told Robert that we would see him at the church and that God was so happy that he was coming!

As I left and drove back home, I told the Lord, "Yes, I believe you, my brother Robert will come. I have complete faith in you. He will come!"

I went on back home. I was so happy as I told everyone Robert was coming to church. The Lord had assured me that Robert would be there! My husband, Bob, and I and all the rest of the persons who were going with us crowded into the truck and cars, and we left for church. I wasn't worried, why should I be? Not with God in my corner! Praise God! He is an exciting God!

As we pulled into the church's parking lot, there was my brother driving in. I shouted, "Praise you Lord, and thank you."

After we parked, we all went into the church. This was only our second Sunday night at this church. For some unknown reason, God had us all sitting in different places. I sat with my dear friend Ellen and my sister-in-law Sherri. Ellen's husband Don sat across the aisle from us. He is blind and a diabetic. A wonderful man who loves the Lord so much too! My husband, Bob, my brother, Robert, and our nephew, Jeff, sat two rows ahead of us.

Boy, oh boy, was God's spirit ever in church that night. It was so wonderful! The sermon was directed at all of us; it was so full of love and truth. I kept feeling like shouting for joy. I could feel God's love all around us.

When the altar call came, the minister asked anyone who wanted to come forward and stand down front. (I've not seen the minister ever do that since either, asking persons to come and stand at the altar.) Well, I had been praying for God to touch all my loved ones. All at once, there went Ellen down the aisle and then went Sherri. I whispered to my Jesus, "Thank you, Jesus!" I had hoped my husband Bob would go, and in that split second, there went Bob down front. Then the next minute, there went my brother, Robert!

I tell you it was so glorious watching my loved ones go down to God's altar. I had to rush across the aisle and tell Don that they had all gone down to the altar. I went back and sat down. Then Don leaned across the aisle and asked me to help him go down to the altar as he wanted to be with Bob and Robert. Well, let me tell you, I took him all right. I think he and I just glided down that aisle so fast. I don't even think our feet touched the ground. Praise the Lord! Praise His work to all my loved ones! Faith can move the highest mountains, and believe me, I have faith in our dear Lord Jesus and our most precious Father of Heaven. In Romans 10:17 it says, "So then faith cometh by hearing, and hearing by the word of God." I love this scripture.

The one verse of the Bible that most makes me think of my dear friend Ellen is Philippians 1:2–3 that states, "Grace be unto you, and peace from God our Father, and from the Lord Jesus Christ. I thank my God upon every remembrance of you." I see Ellen's face every time I read that verse.

Thank you, Lord for keeping the "door to heaven open"! My prayer is that all will enter through that holy door!

A few days later, Sherri, my sister-in-law, and I agreed we were going to pray for one of her sons. His name is Scott. He is one of those beautiful young persons out there in the world—lost but he is searching. There are such terrible things going on in the world; drugs, murder, and robberies are just among a few of the horrible things. So we all have to at least try to reach those lost souls out there. Do something people; if you are reading this, do something for the love of God! Anyway, we prayed for the Lord to help Scott and to please touch Scott in some way so that Scott would know that God is real. One morning I was in the kitchen fixing myself a bowl of cereal (with a banana I might add), and the Lord spoke to my heart in that beautiful small still voice. And the Lord told me to take and pick out a big, beautiful golden banana out of the fruit bowl and take it to Scott.

I laughed and said, "You've got to be kidding, Lord."

And God told me, "No, I am not kidding, tell Scott the banana is a gift from me and laugh all you want to just do as I ask."

I laughed and I laughed for a full fifteen minutes or so, and then I said, "Okay, Lord, I will do it, but God you sure are funny, you do make me laugh!" I laughed for pure joy, and I laughed all day long off and on.

I thought to myself, *No one could ever say God doesn't have a great sense of humor!* God kept me busy all day doing His work. I love it. I love it! I kept telling everyone not to touch Scott's banana. I planned on taking it to Scott that night after supper. Then I remembered Scott's mom, Sherri, and her older son, Jeff, and her youngest son, Johnny Raye, were going to come over that evening, and we were all going to a friend's house—her name is Nadine.

When Sherri came, I explained what the Lord had told me about giving Scott that banana. I told Sherri that she could take it and give it to Scott instead. I still had not learned that when God told me to do something, He meant for me to do it. But thank God, I have learned. So anyhow, Bob and I together with Sherri, her two sons, our son Mike, his girlfriend Karrie, and a lovely girl named Julie and her sister all went over to Nadine's house to watch a Christian movie.

Just before we left, Mike, our son, had come into the kitchen and he asked me, "Mom, why does God want you to take this banana to Scott?"

I told him, "I really don't know, all I know is that it is to go to Scott!"

And Mike told me, "Mom if you don't tell me the real reason God wants Scott to have this banana, I am going to eat the banana!"

I looked at Mike and told him I would knock his block off if he ate that banana. I am small, and Mike is tall. Mike laughed. What a beautiful laugh he has.

He then said, "Okay, Mom, you take it and give it to Scott! But that is a funny thing God wants you to do!"

I agreed—it was funny. Anyhow, after the movie, we all came back to our house. Julie's sister told Sherri that she would take her and her two sons home. Another friend named Ruth was with us too. I told Ruth I would take her home after she drank her coffee.

After Sherri and everyone else had left, Mike came running into the other room, "Oh no, Mom, you forgot to give the banana to Sherri to give to Scott!" he said to me.

"Oh no, well, I guess God wants me to give the banana to Scott myself. I don't understand why I have to do it but, I will go anyway!" I said to Mike and Ruth.

Mike tried to talk me out of going by telling me how much gas I would be wasting by driving all the way to Sherri's place. Sherri and her sons lived about fifteen miles away, way out in the country in an old trailer. It is peaceful way out there. I had hoped to rest but God had other plans. Isn't God good?

Bob was sitting in the other room and he said, "Let her go, she will go no matter what!" I tried to explain to them how I had to go because the Lord wanted me to, not because I chose to go.

Mike laughed again. "Go, but be careful driving alone!"

Ruth spoke up and said she would ride with me and then I could take her home after. So Ruth and I drove all the way out to Sherri's place. When we got there, Ruth said she would wait out in the truck.

I knocked on the door, and Jeff came to the door, and he was surprised to see me so soon; I asked him if Scott was there. He told me yes Scott was in the kitchen. I called to Scott, and we met in the doorway of the kitchen.

I told him, "Scott, bless your heart, this banana is a gift from God!" And I handed him the banana.

Scott looked at that banana and he looked at me and he said, "How did you know? How did you know?"

I asked him, "How did I know what?"

He just stared and repeated, "How did you know? How could you know that for some strange reason, all day long, I have wanted a banana and I don't even care for fruit? I have felt that I just have to have a banana! The feeling has been so strong, I can't ever remember wanting something so bad in my whole life!" Scott worked at the fruit sheds. And he continued to talk, "This man came into the yard this afternoon with a whole truckload of bananas! I tried and tried to get him to give me a banana. I even begged him but he told me no way, he would not give me a banana. And here you come all this way, late at night, and you give me this banana. How in the world did you know?"

I told him, "Scott, I did not know, but God knew and he cared enough about you!" Then I said that I had to go.

Sherri who had been standing there spoke up and said, "I'm not laughing."

I told them, "Go ahead and laugh, God wants you to laugh. Isn't God wonderful?"

It is great what miracles God can do. I left with Scott standing in the doorway of the trailer, waving that banana and shouting, "Thank you, thank you." He had a big, bright, beautiful smile on his face. I will always remember him smiling and waving that banana.

When I got in the truck, I kept saying, "Thank you, God. Praise you. You are so good." Ruth asked me what had happened, and I told her. Wasn't God wonderful? You see, God doesn't tell me why He wants me to do these things. I do them because I know He has a reason. I have complete faith and belief. I will never question Him again. Scott had asked me why did God want him to have that banana, and I told him truthfully, "I don't know!" I just do as God asks me; I don't question Him. So that banana miracle is between our nephew Scott and God. Praise God!

After I got home that night, Mike was sitting up waiting for me. He asked me what happened and I told him. He laughed softly and lay down on the sofa and promptly fell asleep.

A few days later, I was mopping the kitchen floor. I was praying to the Lord. "Lord, you know we agree to let this house go and let you lead us where you want us to go, but please let it be a place where I can have a few chickens, a duck or two, and maybe some rabbits. I'm not sure about the rabbits, but I know I want some chickens and the ducks." With these words I heard a duck quacking outside. I threw my mop down and ran outside and stood looking up at the sky, and I heard the duck's quack, very loudly this time. I didn't see anything, but I felt a beautiful peacefulness whelming up in my heart. I whispered, smiling, "does this mean our next place we'll be able to have ducks? Thank you, Lord."

Boy, was I happy all the rest of that day. You see, no one has any ducks in that whole neighborhood. God is so good.

Of course I told everyone who would listen what had happened. The next morning, I was telling our son, Mike, about the duck's quacking.

Mike smiled and told me, "Mom, there are no ducks here in this neighborhood!"

I told him, "If God wants there to be a duck in this neighborhood, He will put one here. I heard God's duck, not just once, but twice!"

I poured myself a cup of coffee and got the morning newspaper and sat down in my chair. Mike was sitting at my feet on the floor, watching TV. I read the front section of the newspaper—all bad news. God must really be unhappy with this old world. Then I came to the metro section of our newspaper. There toward the bottom of the page was this caption: "Duck deposits self on bank roof, finds much of interest."

I yelled, "Praise God, there's my duck!" It's really God's, but He doesn't mind sharing it with me. "There it is, Mike, my duck, praise God's Holy Name!"

Mike grabbed the newspaper out of my hands. He shouted, "Where, Mom, where is it?"

We both read the article together. The article told how the duck was noticed on the rooftop of a big bank building here on Chester Avenue in our town of Bakersfield, California, and how the officials of the bank refused to call the animal shelter because it had captured the hearts of the employees who climbed up on the roof to feed the duck. The employees even named the duck "Ira Bucks." The vice president of the bank said the duck seemed to have a mind of its own because whenever they tried to chase it away, it refused to leave and just keeps coming back to roost on the edge of the bank's roof. Ira sits and peers down on customers waiting at the drive-up teller. Ira was there for about seven days. Ira gave a lot of joy to the people who drove up to see him.

Mike said to me, "Mom, how do you know that duck is the same duck you heard yesterday here in our own yard? That bank is three or four miles or more from here. How did the duck get from here clear over to that bank?"

I told Mike, "The Lord put that duck, Ira Bucks, here for me to hear. Then God took the duck to that bank for whatever reason God has."

That duck will be wherever God wants it to be. I know, I just know. Praise God, isn't the Lord wonderful? Mike just laughed his beautiful laugh and went into the other room. Later that afternoon we went out to Sherri's place to visit. I told them what God had done and how the Lord had put that duck on that bank building. Johnny Raye, Sherri's youngest son, told us he wanted to see the duck. I told him to pray real hard and if it is God's will, you will get to see Ira Bucks.

Sherri and Johnny Raye came home to our house to stay all night with us so that they could go to church the next day. On the way home, we drove by the bank but it was dark, and we couldn't see the duck.

During the night, the Lord woke me up to read from the Bible. That happens quite a lot, praise God! The life Lord spoke to my heart that I was to leave thirty minutes early before I left to go to church the next morning. I was to take some bread crumbs, an apple, and a bowl for water and go to feed the duck, Ira Bucks! Let me tell you, I was excited. It was hard to go back to sleep the rest of the night. No one was awake the next morning, so I got up and got ready for church by myself, always checking what time it was because I knew I needed to allow thirty extra minutes to go and feed Ira! I took the bowl, bread, and apple and put it all into a bag and I left. I drove to the bank, praising the Lord every mile that I drove! When I got to the bank and pulled into the parking lot, there was Ira, walking slowly back and forth in the parking lot, stopping to peck at something on the ground. I whispered, "Thank you, God, for letting me have this opportunity to visit your precious duck!"

I got slowly out of the truck because I did not want to scare one of God's creatures. Ira just kept on walking back and forth. I walked up to Ira quietly and told Ira, "Bless your heart, Ira. Aren't you beautiful? How God loves you. I brought you something to eat, but you'll have to excuse me because I'm very ignorant about what kind of food ducks eat. God told me to bring you this beautiful bread and an apple, and here is a bowl. I see a water faucet over there, so I will get you some water!"

I went to the water faucet and put water in the bowl and put it right below the faucet on the ground. "Here is some water for you Ira," I said. And I started tearing up small bits of bread and throwing it gently toward Ira. Ira ran straight to it and began eating the bread. Then I had forgotten to bring a knife to cut up the apple so I bit off small chunks of apple—I didn't want Ira to get choked on a piece—and gave these to the duck. Ira ate and ate as I talked. No one ever came; it was just Ira and me and the Lord. Ira was a small, beautiful white duck with an orange-colored beak and golden orange feet. I don't know much about ducks, but she had like a red mask around her beautiful little eyes! She was indeed very, very beautiful, and there was something different about her—something special, I think. I went back and looked inside the truck and found a bag of marshmallows. I don't know how they got there. I took and put tiny bits of marshmallow down on the ground also for Ira. Ira would eat, go get a drink of water from the bowl, and then walk around some more, and she would stop occasionally and cock her little head at me and look at me. Then she would go and eat some more. Up at the window of the drive-up teller, there was a sign that read, "Because of the power failure, please go to the bank over on such and such street. Sorry for the inconvenience."

I said, "Praise God, you know the bank had been closed early Friday, so there hasn't been anyone to feed Ira for the last three days. Thank you for having me come and feed your lovely duck, Ira! Thank you, Lord!"

Then I told Ira, "I have to go now because it is almost time for church to start, and the Lord is trying to teach me to be on time this week! I will be back to feed you again, later! Bless you, Ira, for bringing joy with you. Isn't God good?"

As soon as I said this, Ira turned her little head back and forth and looked at me and started flapping her beautiful wings and flew clear up on the top of the building of the bank. Then she walked out of sight.

Later that afternoon after church, I went home and told everyone about seeing Ira! They were excited too and Johnny Raye said, "Aunt Beth, I want to go and see Ira."

So I told him after lunch we would go and if it was God's will for him and his Mom to see Ira, then Ira would still be at the bank.

When the time came to leave, I told Sherri and Johnny Raye, "Now, when we get almost there to the bank, start praying to God, and tell God you believe that you will get to see the duck." Just before we turned the corner before the bank, I looked over across from me, and I could see Sherri and Johnny Raye praying fervently. Bless their hearts!

When we got to the bank, Ira was perched up on the top of the drive-thru area, but she wouldn't come down. Johnny talked to her anyway and put more bread down. Sherri loved the duck too. She remarked how unusual it looked. So that was a lovely day, being able to feed the Lord's beautiful duck. I went back two more times during the week. The last time I took food but I didn't see her. I prayed for God to watch over Ira Bucks wherever she was.

A few days later, the Lord spoke to my heart again that we were to get my brother Robert a Bible. Well the Lord had told us that we were to economize and that we were going to let our house go, and go where He led us.

I asked the Lord, "Where am I going to get money for Robert's Bible, Lord?"

The Lord told me I was to go to the Christian Book Store and tell them that He sent me and that I needed a cheap Bible—not a free Bible—and that we were economizing and not buying any Christmas presents or even sending Christmas cards out. Well, I was nervous because it is easy to witness to your friends and loved ones, but this time I was to stand in front of a perfect stranger and tell that stranger that God sent me for a cheap Bible, not a free Bible but a cheap one!

Well let me tell you my friends, that was the hardest thing that I had ever had to do! I was told to ask for the manager of the store when I went in and I was to go by myself.

That night, I got in the truck and I prayed and I said to the Lord, "Lord, I can't do this. I am weak, but you are strong. So please go with me and you're going to have to talk through me, because I don't know what to say or do."

When I got to the store, I sat outside for a few minutes, and then I said, "I am going, Lord, but please go with me!"

When I got inside, I looked around, because I did not know who I was supposed to talk to, so I wandered around for a few minutes. Then I went over to a young clerk in the record department. The clerk looked at me and asked if he could help me. I took a deep breath and asked him for the manager. He told me there wasn't a manager at night.

I thought, *Now Lord, what do I do?*

So I took another deep breath and said in a big rush, "God sent me to get a Bible for my brother. I'm to ask for a cheap Bible, not free just cheap! My brother is a lost soul and needs a Bible. The Lord wants our family to economize this Christmas and we are not sending any Christmas cards nor are we buying any Christmas presents either. So, bless your heart. I need a cheap, not free, just a cheap Bible."

The clerk looked at me and smiled and told me, "Go over to the Bible department and tell them exactly the same words that you've just told me!"

I thanked him and walked away slowly, thinking, *Lord, you didn't tell me I was going to have to say those words to two people! Please be with me again!*

I must admit I walked very, very slowly. Do you know how hard it is to look someone in the eye and tell them God sent you? When I got over to the Bible section, I looked around and could see Bibles in boxes on huge shelves all over the place. I got a swift look at some of the prices and I thought to myself, *Lord, I can't pay any of these prices!*

There was a young lady behind the counter and she asked me if she could help me. So, I once again took a deep breath and all the words came tumbling out again. I once again explained how the Lord has sent me and He had told me to tell them that I needed a cheap, not free, Bible for my troubled brother and how we were economizing also for the Lord this Christmas.

She looked at me and asked me, "What do you want me to do?"

I told her I needed her to help me find a cheap Bible for my brother, Robert. She came out on the floor and took me over to a far corner and there stood a box of Bibles. She told me these were the cheapest Bibles that they had. She opened one of the boxes and showed me—it was just an ordinary Bible. She told me those cost $16.95. I shook my head and told her that wasn't cheap enough.

She smiled, put the Bible down, and told me there was a Bible that churches sometimes buy for their missionaries, but it was only a few dollars cheaper.

I told her, "Let's look at those Bibles," thinking, *Lord, I still do not have $14 or $15 either.*

We walked over to this huge rack of boxed Bibles, and she kept looking and looking. Of course, I did not know what she was looking for so I just stood there.

She said, "There doesn't seem to be any of those Bibles." Then all of a sudden she said, "Now, that is strange."

And I started smiling, because I know God was going to do a miracle.

She spoke up and said, "Now, where did those Bibles come from?" She turned to me and told me, "There are two Bibles sitting here in the middle of this rack, and they are not in boxes, and we cannot sell a Bible without a box, not at the normal price. Here is a blue Bible and a nice brown Bible. You can have one of these for $5.95. Is that cheap enough?"

I smiled very broadly, I must admit, and said, "Thank you, Lord!" I softly told her, "Bless your heart; that is the perfect price!" And I looked at both of the Bibles and picked the beautiful, beautiful, brown Bible! It was so beautiful and it actually seemed to glow, very softly. I know God was very, very pleased.

She put the other Bible back on the shelf. Then she asked me, "Now, wouldn't you like to have it engraved?"

I shook my head and told her, "No thank you, the Lord says $5.95 is the right price."

She looked at the Bible and down at the floor, and then she looked up and smiled and said, "Now, wouldn't you really, really like to have it engraved? It's free. There is no charge to you."

I felt like shouting for joy, but all I could do was shake my head up and down! Wasn't God being wonderful?

She had me fill out a card with my brother's name. I tell you, I felt like I was way up in heaven with Jesus and my Heavenly Father—I was so happy. I may have been standing there, but my heart was up with my Jesus! After she was through engraving, she brought the Bible to show me how beautiful it looked. She acted like she was carrying a handful of gold. So carefully and gently she held that Bible.

She smiled and asked me, "Isn't it beautiful?"

And I yelled, "Praise God! Thank you and bless your heart. Yes, it is beautiful!" I paid $5.95 plus tax for that beautiful Bible for my brother, Robert. I was praising the Lord all the way home. Boy, was I excited.

When I showed everyone, they said there was no way I could get a beautiful Bible like that for only $5.95 plus tax. I laughed and told them, "When God is with you and helping you, anything is possible. Isn't God good?"

So that is how I got a cheap Bible, not free but cheap for my brother Robert. God was teaching me to stand up on my two feet and not to be afraid to praise Him. Boy, oh, boy, is it fun to learn lessons from the Lord. He is a wonderful teacher, And I just have to add, there is something very special and very beautiful about that Bible.

A few days later, our cesspool in our backyard filled up, and we had to have it pumped. The people pumped it and that took our last few dollars. A few days later, the cesspool backed up again, and the company found out that they had not pumped both of the tanks. (They hadn't been able to find one of the tanks, so they just figured it was an old house and that it only had one tank.) Well, the man told me over the phone that he would have to charge us for digging to find the other tank, but if someone dug the hole, there would not be any more cost. They could not come back until next morning. By then it was getting late, and I knew my husband, Bob, would not get home until after dark. So I prayed and asked the Lord what to do. The Lord told me to dig, so I dug. I. did not know where to dig. I was just guessing. With each shovel full of dirt and gunk, I kept praising the Lord. The more I dug, the more I praised the Lord. I got so excited praising the Lord that when I finally looked up, I realized I had dug a hole five or six feet!

I asked the Lord, "Wouldn't he think that maybe I had dug the hole too deep?"

When Bob came home and came in the backyard, he looked at that hole and he looked at me, and he started laughing. "What in the world are you doing?"

I told him how I knew he would be tired when he got home so I was just trying to help so that he wouldn't have to dig. I told him that the cesspool men would be there first thing in the morning. Besides he went to work at 4:30 a.m. and he didn't have time to dig. Our son, Mike, was working two jobs. So that left me to dig. I told him how each time I dug a shovel of dirt and gunk I just kept praising the Lord. So it wasn't too bad digging for the Lord.

Bob looked at the hole again and kept on laughing as he told me, "Honey, that was nice that you wanted to keep me from having to dig, and I hate to tell you this, but, you have dug way too deep. You did not need to dig but a couple of feet."

Well, what could I do? I had already dug that big hole. Oh, well, I had fun praising the Lord anyway.

The next morning the cesspool man came and when I went out to meet him, he asked me who had dug that great big hole. I sheepishly told him how I had been so excited praising the Lord that I guessed I had gotten carried away.

He laughed and laughed and said, "Yes, I guess you did!"

All during this month, the Lord had started telling me to record gospel tapes of a few records that I had. Pretty soon the Lord had given me a whole list of names to make tapes for. First of all, let me tell you, all I know about a stereo is how to put the record on, or the tape in the slot, and how to turn the radio off and on. I had never ever even thought of taping and recording. I didn't even know what to do at all! Thank heavens I do know how to follow directions good. Our son, Mike, showed me how to record from another tape or from a record.

I had lots of fun. When you are doing something for the Lord, you tend to get so excited. The Lord told me I was to record and to make sure that I put the person's name on the tapes. I followed my list of names, and then halfway through, I decided I liked that tape, so I would keep it for myself and add that person's name to the bottom of the list that the Lord had given me. But when I played the tape back, it was all garbled. I told the Lord that I was sorry and to forgive me for being selfish, and I erased that person's name from the bottom of the list and put their name on that tape. Then I asked God if that was okay now and I played the tape again, and it played perfect. Wasn't God funny?

I even gave my sister-in-law Sherri a tape, and boy, was she excited. She loved it, and we had given her an old portable cassette player to play the tape on. A few days after we gave Sherri the tape (it had her name on it), she called me and asked me if we would feel bad if she gave her tape to her friend, Bernice. She explained how she dearly loved the tape, but something was telling her to give it to Bernice. I told Sherri how sweet that was of her, wanting to share like that. And I told her to go ahead and that I would tape her another tape during the weekend. After she hung up the phone, I thought that it was a wonderful gesture for Sherri to give Bernice that tape. I forgot about it until the next day. Sherri called us and this is what she told us had happened the night before. Sherri had given Bernice the tape and in return Bernice had given Sherri a tape of Cristy Lane. Sherri played her new tape after Bernice left. Bernice had told Sherri that she would stop by once more to see her on the way back to go home. Bernice lives in Tehachapi, which is approximately thirty-five miles from Bakersfield.

Four or five hours later, Bernice came back and pulled into Sherri's yard and came inside the trailer. The first thing Bernice said was, "Sherri, why in the world did you give me a blank tape? I tried and tried to play the tape, and there is nothing on that tape at all."

Sherri told her she was sorry that the tape hadn't played for her. Bernice told her that she had to get home because a storm was coming in, and could she please give her Cristy Lane tape back? Bernice gave Sherri her tape back and then left to go back to Tehachapi. Well, Sherri felt real sad because she thought something must have happened to the tape for it not to play. She went on and fixed supper and afterward Sherri decided to read her Bible, and something told her to put her tape in her cassette machine and play it. So she thought, *Well, I guess I'll just try it.* And guess what? It played! It played just perfect! Isn't God grand?

When Sherri told me that, I shouted, "Praise God, Sherri! That is beautiful. I never dreamed that you weren't supposed to give the tape away. I know the Lord said to put your name on it. I didn't know it mattered. Don't you see, God wanted you to have that tape. It has your name on it. So don't give it away again." Sherri assured me she wouldn't.

So I made sure from then on, I shared with everyone I gave a tape to about what had happened with Sherri's tape. I even taped Bernice a tape, with her name on it, and sent it to her.

About this time also, our son, Mike, wanted to throw a birthday party for his girlfriend, Karrie. I told him we were going to be gone that whole afternoon and evening. I told him that I would make some potato salad and baked beans but that we were low on money and that was all we could do.

During the week before the birthday party, I was reading a book, *The Valley of Vision* by Betsy Patterson. I loved that book; it was so inspiring. I remember when I was in high school, in English class, how I used to write short funny stories. I had never given any thought to trying to write now. God spoke to me and spoke to me, all through that entire book, how he wanted me to write a book and tell His people a few things and most of all I was to tell all mankind: "The door to heaven is still open, tell the people to come home!"

I thought, *Here I am forty years old, but this Betsy Patterson did it with the good Lord helping her all the time.* So I told the Lord, "I will write your book. Lord, but you know how ignorant of writing a book I am, I do not know the first thing of what to do. I will be leaning on you, God, all the time and you will have to lead me and guide me on what to do."

It was as if I felt (as I sat there in my chair) a soft hand gently patting me on the head and I heard the beautiful voice of the Lord telling me, "My child, I will be beside you always and I will help you. After all, haven't I always been there for you?"

I joyfully told the Lord, "Yes you were there all the time and I never knew! Thank you, Lord for being with me and not forsaking me!"

As the Lord gave me the title of the book, I wrote it down. And it stayed put away for quite a while. The Lord had lots of lessons for me to learn. Because you know, God has a reason and a season for everything. It is hard sometimes to be patient. The Lord has to stop and teach us patience every once in a while.

So came the morning of Mike's birthday party for Karrie.

Mike came home and told me, "Mom, what am I going to do? My car broke down, and I had to get it fixed. Then I remembered I had not bought the hamburger. So I went to the store and this is all the hamburger I could buy." I looked at his two small packages of hamburger. I think each package was one pound a piece.

I told Mike, "Son, that is not enough hamburger for your party. We do not have any money to help you either. How many people have you invited?"

Mike said he had invited twenty people.

I said, "Oh no, there certainly isn't enough hamburger for twenty big, strong, young people!"

Then I remembered how in Betsy Patterson's book when she did not have enough ingredients for her fruitcakes, she trusted in the Lord and the Lord had doubled her recipe. So I smiled and told Mike to give me his hamburger and to go away because God was going to do a miracle.

Mike asked me, "What are you going to do Mom?"

I told him, "Mike, I am not going to do anything. God is the one who is going to do the miracle! Remember how I told you what God did for Betsy Patterson in her book, with her fruitcakes?"

Mike said, "Mom, that was in a book!"

I told him, "We only have to trust in the Lord, and have faith! Don't worry, Mike!"

So Mike left, and I got down on my hands and knees and I prayed and I told the Lord, "Lord, I trust, I believe, and I have faith in you, even if the rest of them don't yet, it's okay. I will believe enough for all of them. Then when you are ready, you can touch them and help them to believe! But Lord, I don't understand why it is so hard for all of the people to believe in you. It is so easy—you are so wonderful! Anyway, please we need a small miracle. Mike needs lots of hamburgers for Karrie's birthday party. So will you please make the hamburger double or triple? I thank you, Lord, for what you are about to do!"

I got up and the Lord spoke to my heart and told me, "My child, I will fix it for you!"

I got two big bowls out like the Lord told me to do, and I mixed in the ingredients the Lord told me to mix. Afterward, I thought, *Lord, it still doesn't look like enough to feed everyone, but I am still trusting you.*

The Lord told me, "Make the patties for the hamburgers and watch what happens."

Well, I got some flat cookie sheets out on the counter and I began to shape round patties with my hands, and then I flattened them out and placed them on the cookie sheet. Praise God! I kept making patties. I tell you, I didn't think I was ever going to get to the end of the hamburger. Every time I thought I was at the end of the bowl, I looked inside and there was plenty of hamburger still left. So with that little bit of hamburger, God made almost forty hamburgers. Nice big and juicy ones too! God is so good!

When Mike came home a few hours later, I was still making the patties, and Mike could not believe how many patties the Lord had made! I told Mike, "See what God has done, look at all your hamburger patties. Now isn't that a good miracle that God has done?"

And Mike laughed and agreed it certainly was. They had a real nice birthday party and plenty of hamburgers. Thanks to God's miracle! Praise God!

The next day we had a real bad windstorm. After the storm ended, we called Sherri to check up on them and make sure they were all okay. Sherri told us that the wind had blown the roof off of the trailer half off and that Jeff her eldest son was trying to help some other men put the roof back on again. They did get it back on, but it leaked all over the place. And their butane tank was messed up too, so they could not cook. Also they were worried about the wiring.

When Bob came home from work a bit later, I told him what had happened out at Sherri's trailer. We talked it over and decided to just trust the Lord, completely, and go out and bring Sherri and her three sons in to live with us for as long as they needed to stay.

But Bob told me, "We do not have enough money to feed all of us," with Sherri, her three sons, Bob and I, our daughter Rebecca (she's eighteen years old), our son Mike (he's twenty years old), and another young lady, named Julie (she's eighteen years old too), so that made nine of us. We will really have to trust in the Lord to feed all of us. So we went out to their trailer and brought them all to our house. So for almost two weeks, during the Christmas season, we had a whole houseful of people.

But God was so good to us. I fixed enough food, just as if there were five of us eating, and all nine of us always ate until we were full, and there even was always a tiny bit of food left over after each meal. All we have to do is put our trust completely in the Lord. It may seem sort of hard at first, but it gets easier the more you place your trust in the Lord.

But anyway this was why Sherri and her family were staying with us. That night they were at our house, and all of us finally got to go to sleep. We were all so tired. During the night, I am awakened from my slumber by the joyous singing of the words, "Come on ring those bells, light those Christmas trees / Jesus is the King! Born for you and me!" Jesus gives me a blessing that feels so wondrous; it is hard to find the words to write of it (but I will try). He fills me with unspeakable joy and peace.

He comforts me and gives me the beautiful gift of hope for all mankind. Praise God, praise His wondrous name! My heart has been troubled for all the lost souls; they must be saved. For they are our

Father's beloved children. I feel utter peace and contentment as God speaks softly to me. As I am lying in bed next to my beloved husband, God whispers gently in my mind and heart I am with Him—I feel as if I am with Him. I can see and feel Him. As He goes from soul to soul, He places His hand on them oh so gently and God blesses each and every one of them as they lay sleeping.

Oh, the beauty of it all! I know I am lying in bed, but it is as if I am right beside the Lord, gliding softly from my loved ones to the souls sleeping in our city.

I can look down below and see the city lights, yet I can see the beautiful souls sleeping too. The Lord sees their hearts as they sleep. He touches them once again, but this time His mighty hand reaches out like a small white dove, and He touches their hearts. I see Him as He does this thing, and yet I feel as if I am there beside our Heavenly Father! The Lord rushes from heart to heart, preparing them. I see *God* touching all of my loved ones in our house as they lay sleeping! How glorious this experience is. I have never had anything so beautiful happen to me.

Then I arose from bed and saw the clock showed the time to be 3:30 a.m., and God places the need in my heart to get up from my bed and read Psalms 18–30 from my Bible.

As I walked through the living room to go into the kitchen with my Bible, Sherri was sleeping on the floor, and she sat straight up and asked me, "What are you doing?"

I smiled and softly told her, "Go back to sleep, Sherri. God is blessing all of you. It is so beautiful, and now I am going to read the Bible."

Sherri smiled and said, "Okay!" and laid back down and promptly went back to sleep. The next day she says she didn't remember any of this. Anyway I read all those chapters of Psalms, and how comforting these verses in the Bible are. I begin yet another lap on my glorious journey for God as I read His comforting words. I even have to put my thoughts of *God* in writing in the margins of my Bible, as my dear spiritual friend Ellen has shown me to do.

How wise God is. He sends us the friends we need, at just the right time, when He knows our very souls are starved for a friend.

After I finish reading and writing, I go back to sleep some more. But alas I cannot; God fills my very heart and mind with such wondrous thoughts. And I quietly ask *God* to help my physical body to rest for the new day. But I cannot! I cannot rest!'

Praise *God*, He wants me to arise and write once more.

My heart fills with joy, because I like nothing better than to feel Him use me as His vessel. I will write and I will talk as He directs me. "In Jesus's name!" Also I must ready my house in preparation for a glorious new day. I do the few chores with a gladdened heart! For God is preparing our house to follow in the worship of our Almighty God. Praise the Lord!

I do not worry any longer over my sleeping loved ones. The fears and threats against their very souls that I felt a few weeks ago are completely washed away by God.

God is so merciful toward mankind. I had wanted to sleep and stay in that nice warm bed, but a beautiful voice whispered my name, "Beth, arise and do my bidding, now!"

I am glad I arose, because God is my protector and my shield. He fills my very heart and soul with such peace that it is hard to imagine anything being so beautiful.

I will walk in the path that God has directed me, forever and ever. I'll never err from His pathway. Mankind must unite in love and hope. Do not let the wicked separate you.

I am overcome with all the blessings that God has bestowed on me tonight, or I guess I should say morning.

Before my hand stops for now, I see a man, a woman, and a child.

Do not lament, and do not feel sad. This child is born of love.

Now I am weary and I will lay my pen down and go to rest for a while until God awakens me in a few hours to a new and glorious morning. Goodnight, sweet dreams too all!

The next morning after I had gotten up, I saw that I had been writing again. I was overwhelmed by the beauty of my experience that I had written! *God* is very, very precious! I wrote the last four and a half pages exactly as it were written down that night. I've never experienced a night like that since. I always say that was the night that the Lord came to visit. A few days later, Sherri wanted to go back out to her trailer and stay for a few days to try to get things cleaned up.

After they left, the next day we helped our dear friends Don and Ellen move to Dinuba, California. Coming back home, I felt so sad; we knew we would see each other again, but it still felt extra sad. So when we got home, I prayed for the Lord to keep me real busy doing something for Him, so I wouldn't have time to feel sad. The next morning as I was watching the news on television, the station showed the homeless people over on Baker Street.

And I got down on my knees right there and prayed, "Lord, I want to do something for those people. I know I am only one person, but please help us to do something. I don't care whatever you want us to do—we'll do it!" I know each year they show these poor people on television, around Christmas time, because people's hearts are more generous at Christmas time. But why can't people care about the homeless all year round, not just during Christmas? Each year before I did just like so many other people have done, I thought, *How sad*, and yet, I did nothing. So this year I wanted to do something.

And the Lord spoke to me in His beautiful small still voice that He wanted our family to gather clothing for the homeless people over on Baker Street and also the Lord said we were not to buy any Christmas presents this Christmas nor send any Christmas cards either. The Lord said He would show us the true meaning of Christmas. (And praise God! That is what happened.)

I got so excited. At last we were going to do something for God's people, instead of sitting back and doing nothing.

Blessed God, He is so good!

Now let me go on with this story about *the miracle lady*. A few weeks earlier, we had taken Sherri and Johnny Raye (Sherri's youngest son) out with us to visit our sweet friend Nadine. Whenever we take anybody with us in the truck, they usually have to ride in the back of the truck. And it can get mighty cold in the winter time.

Sherri did not have a coat so she rode in the front of the truck this time, but after we visited and we got ready to go home, Nadine asked Sherri, "Sherri, honey, where is your coat?" (It was really cold that particular night.)

Sherri told her that she didn't have a coat, and Nadine went into her spare bedroom. She came out carrying a light green coat and told Sherri, "Sherri, this coat belonged to my mother. She has been dead for almost ten years now. All of her clothes are still hanging in my spare closet. You may have her coat—it is nice and warm! Sometimes I feel guilty that all her clothes are hanging in the closet, not doing anyone any good!"

Sherri tried the coat on, but it didn't fit her very well. She thanked Nadine anyway.

Nadine told her, "Sherri, I can see the coat doesn't fit you very good, so if you know anyone who needs a coat, then you just give it to that person, okay?"

So Sherri assured Nadine that she would. Anyhow that is how Sherri came to receive that special coat.

So to get back to the day, I was watching television and the station was showing the plight of the homeless people that live over on Baker Street in our city of Bakersfield.

As I watched the news, I felt such an overwhelming feeling of sadness for them.

I thought, *Bless their hearts, Lord, how terrible for them!*

"Let us do something for your poor homeless people," I prayed.

I don't want to just sit back in the pews at church and do nothing. I want to do something for you. And when the Lord revealed to me about gathering the clothes for the homeless again I say, "Boy, oh boy, did I feel excited!" And I decided to call Sherri to tell her what *God* wanted us to do.

As Sherri listened to me, I asked Sherri if she had heard me as she was so quiet. And this is what Sherri said to me, "Thank God, thank God, now maybe I can find my lady!"

I asked her, "Sherri, what lady?"

Sherri said, "You know that coat that Nadine gave me? Well ever since she gave me that coat, for the last few weeks the Lord has put an image of a bent-over little old lady, digging through a big trash bin. I see a shopping cart (like at the grocery stores) with a home-made basket tied to the bottom.

But I can't see her face or the color of her hair. And no matter if I am awake or asleep, I see this image of this little old lady, and God tells me I am to find this lady and give her that coat because she is so cold.

Sherri added, "I didn't know how in a million years I was ever going to be able to find this lady, and I have been frantic!"

I asked Sherri why she hadn't told us since we had seen her regularly during the last few weeks?

But Sherri said she had never had anything like this happen to her before. And it frightened her a little; also she wasn't sure anyone would believe her.

I told her, "Sherri, praise God. When it's time, the Lord will help us find your lady! This is beautiful!"

So we were all excited, and we ended up with a whole truckload of clothes for the homeless people.

We asked everyone we saw to donate clothes for the homeless, and we were pleased with the results of people's generosity. During this time, Sherri and her family came back to stay at our house, because it was raining a bit and her trailer was leaking real bad. Anyway we had bagged all the clothes nice and neat in clean trash bags.

The Lord had told me how we were to deliver the clothes and how I was to give His people a message.

Finally the night came for us to deliver the clothes. I told Sherri to make sure she didn't put the special coat in with the rest of the homeless person's clothes!

And we prepared to take the clothes over to the people on Baker Street. So Bob, my husband, Sherri, her friend Ruth, Sherri's youngest son Johnny Raye, and I all piled into the truck. Bob, Johnny Raye, and I rode inside the truck, and Ruth and Sherri rode in the back of the truck on top of all the bags of clothes. Boy, were we a sight!

I told Bob we were to go to the little park on Baker Street. So we drove to the other side of town and we pulled up by the park.

And Bob asked me, "What are we supposed to do, now?"

The park was empty except for two Spanish-looking men sitting on a park bench, by the curb. As I looked at them, I told Bob, "Well, the Lord said there would be a spokesman for His people here, and I know what to say, but God is being funny again, there are two men here instead of one man!" "But I will go over to the bench and the Lord will tell me what to say!"

Bob told me they would all wait in the truck. So I got out and walked up to the two Spanish-looking men sitting on the bench. And I asked them if they spoke English.

One man shook his head and said, "No!"

But the other man spoke up, and he said, "I do!"

So I said to him, "Well, bless your hearts, you must be the spokesman for the homeless people that the Lord said would be here, so I will tell you what the Lord says to tell you. The Lord wanted our family to gather clothing for all of you homeless people here on Baker Street."

"And so we have gathered a whole truck full of clothes for all of you, in our dear Savior's name! And God says there is to be no fighting or fussing between all of you. You are all to share the clothes; if you have friends who need something, you are to share with them. And even if you don't know the people but you know of one of God's people that need something, you are to share with them. And God says to tell you He loves all of you. There is hope for all of you. So don't stop dreaming or hoping—do not give up! Because there is hope for all of you. And God cares about you. You are not forgotten. But most of all, the Lord cares and He loves you."

"And there are people out here in this city—we care for you too."

As I was talking, these two men both stood there with tears streaming down their beautiful careworn faces.

And the one man said, "I do believe in God. I do believe in God! This is a miracle! This is the best Christmas we've ever had! I do believe in God!"

And he hugged me, the tears still streaming down his dear sweet face. And I hugged him too as I felt God's love envelope all three of us. Then the man spoke to the other man and asked if they could help unload the truck. I told them that would be very nice. Then praise God, out of nowhere there came a whole crowd of men. And they quietly offered to help Bob and Sherri unload the truck. And they were so quiet and peaceful and above all so beautiful. I stood to the side and watched all of them.

And I whispered, silently in my heart, "Thank you, Lord, for allowing us to share the miracle You are doing tonight."

There was no pushing, no shoving, or no tearing of the bags. They sat all the bags in the middle of the park, so gently. Some of them were down on their hands and knees, praying; tears falling down their dear faces; others were simply standing quietly, patting the bags.

Lord, they were so beautiful. And they kept telling us, "Thank you, thank you, this is a miracle! We do believe in God! *Merry Christmas*, to all of you. And please thank all the people who gave us the clothes and blankets."

After the truck was empty, I told Bob, "I need to ask them a question about if they know Sherri's lady, and tell them God's message again, then I'll be ready to go!"

So Bob and Sherri went back and sat in the truck, and I faced all the men this time, and I repeated to them how God loved them and that there was hope for them and all mankind. I told them not to give up because *God* cared about them always and too keep on believing, hoping, and dreaming. Because God says there is hope,

Then I turned to this big beautiful black man and this other Spanish-looking man, and I asked them, "A few weeks ago, a friend of ours gave my sister-in-law, Sherri, a green coat. And it didn't fit her very well. And ever since she was given that coat, the Lord has put in her mind an image of a little, tiny, bent-over, old lady. No matter whether she is awake or asleep, she sees this image of this little old lady. And Sherri can see her digging through a big trash bin, and beside the little old lady is a shopping cart, with a little homemade basket tied to the bottom."

"Sherri cannot see this lady's face or the color of her hair. But the Lord tells Sherri that she is to find this lady and give her the coat, because this little old lady is really, really, cold. Do any of you know of such a lady that fits this description?"

And the two men looked at me, then at each other, and then they both spoke up at the same time saying, "We know her, we know her, but you won't find her out here at nighttime."

"Come back during the day and look for her, you'll find her then. You did not put her coat in with our things, did you?"

And I assured them that we had kept the coat separate, and I thanked them. As we were leaving, they were shouting, "Thank you all, and God bless you and Merry Christmas!"

And we called, "Merry Christmas, and remember God loves you all!" as we drove off.

After we got home, Bob went to bed, and Sherri and I sat around the kitchen table. And Sherri said, "That was so good, so wonderful, what God did tonight!"

And I agreed that it was so beautiful yet so overwhelming and sad, all at the same time. Then I remembered about those men and how they had known Sherri's lady, and I told her what they had said.

Sherri said, "They really knew her?"

And I assured her that they did and that when the time was right, the Lord was going to lead us to her lady.

The next day was Sunday, and after I had gotten home from church, Sherri had stayed home to fix breakfast for everyone, and Bob decided he wanted to take a nap. After we all ate, I told Sherri to get the coat because it was time, and the Lord was going to help us find her lady now. Because now it was time. So Sherri got the coat, and she, Johnny Raye, and I all got in the truck.

And we drove over to Baker Street again. We drove up and down the streets looking for Sherri's lady.

Don't ask me how in the world we thought that we were going to know her—we just knew, without a shadow of a doubt!

We just knew that when we saw Sherri's lady, we would know her. We just knew. So we all drove through the streets and down the alleys. Until, finally I told Sherri, "We are going to have to pull over and pray for the Lord to lead us exactly where He wants us to go."

And Sherri said, "Okay, and I sure am worried about all the gas we must be using."

And I looked at the gas gauge, and I shouted, "Sherri, this is incredible! Look the gas gauge has not moved, not even a little bit!" And you know that even with all the driving we did the rest of the afternoon and going all the way home, we never, I repeat, we never used any gas that whole afternoon. Isn't God good? So we pulled over and we prayed to *God* to please lead us exactly where He wanted us to go.

And Sherri spoke up and said, "I see the color brown in my mind. I don't understand what it means!"

I told her, "Bless your heart, Sherri. God is telling you something, so we will just drive around some more, and He will lead us."

So we drove some more, and as we drove through an alley, there was a woman, all dressed in brown, digging through a large trash bin.

Sherri said, "There's a lady all dressed in brown, but she isn't the lady that I'm supposed to give the coat to."

I said, "Well, that's okay, but why don't you get out and go ask her if she knows your lady anyway?"

So Sherri got out of the truck, and she walked over to the lady and told her, "You may not understand this, but a few weeks ago, I was given a coat that didn't fit me very well, and ever since, God has put in my mind, whether I am awake or asleep, an image of a tiny small, bent-over little old lady. I do not see her face nor the color of her hair, but I see a shopping cart next to her, with a small home-made basket tied to the bottom of the cart. I see her digging through a trash bin.

"The Lord tells me I am to find this little lady and give her this coat because she is very, very, cold! Do you know of such a lady?"

The woman watched Sherri as she talked, and then she looked at the coat that Sherri was carrying and she looked at Sherri again, and told her, "I know her, I know her! She walks up and down the next two streets over from here, every day. She pushes her cart, and she is all bent over because she is old and she has arthritis all through her tiny body! You just drive up and down those two streets, and you'll find her."

Sherri asked the woman in brown, "Well since you know her, maybe you can take the coat and give it to her?"

But the woman in brown shook her head and smiled, "Oh no, I couldn't do that; God wants you to give her the coat! You just go and look for her and you will find her."

Sherri came back to the truck and told Johnny Raye and I what the lady in brown had said.

I told her, "Praise God, Sherri, now the Lord has narrowed it down to two streets. Let's go and find your Lady."

So we went two streets over and drove up and down. After a while, Sherri said, "I don't see her, when are we going to find my lady?"

I told her, "Sherri, don't give up now. The Lord did not bring us this far to let us down. We're going to find your lady, so don't worry!"

So as we drove around the streets, we saw a laundry on Baker Street and I stopped and suggested to Sherri that she go inside and ask the people, if they had seen her lady!

So Sherri went inside the laundry, and there were some people in there washing their clothes. And Sherri spoke to them and asked them if she could talk to them.

Then Sherri explained once again how the Lord had put this image of a bent-over, tiny old lady in her mind, no matter whether she was asleep or awake, digging through a big trash bin, how this little lady had a shopping cart with a small homemade basket tied to the bottom, how Sherri could not see her face or even the color of the little lady's hair, and how the Lord told her she was to find this little old lady and give her this coat—and she showed them the coat—because God told her this little old lady was really, really cold. Well, they looked at her like she was crazy, all except this young girl.

And this young girl stepped forward and told Sherri, "I know her, I know her! She was just here! She lives down on East Kentucky Street in a tiny, little house. I don't know her personally or exactly which house. But you go look for her and you'll find her! And she has lots of cats, and she is just the way you describe her."

And Sherri came running out and told us what the young girl had said.

And I said, "Praise God, Sherri, praise God. Now the Lord has narrowed it down to one street. For sure we are going to find your lady. Get in this truck, and let's go!"

By this time we were so excited; it was like going on a lovely treasure hunt for the Lord. I've never been on a treasure hunt, but this is what I imagine it must feel like to be on one. So we drove up and down Kentucky Street looking for Sherri's lady. We drove through some more alleys and then as we were coming back around a corner off Kentucky Street, Sherri turned toward me talking, and all of a sudden she saw a movement out of the corner of her eye. And Sherri turned her head, and there standing in a little fenced yard was a tiny, small-boned, white-haired, little old Lady.

And Sherri yelled, "There's my lady, there she is! There she is!"

And we were hollering, "Thank you. Lord, thank you, and praise God, praise God!"

By this time we had already driven past the house, so we went back through the alley and pulled up in front of the house! The little old lady had went inside, so we parked in front of the house, and we looked at the house.

And as we looked, we could see this shopping cart, sitting right by the front door! I said to Sherri, "Sherri, Sherri, look, there is her shopping cart, with the little homemade basket tied onto the bottom; it's exactly just as you have been describing it. It's just like God put in your mind. Praise God, Sherri, it's exactly like you said it looked!"

Then Sherri said, "I'm a little scared, what should I do now?"

And I laughed joyfully, "Bless your heart, Sherri, just go up and knock on the door. The Lord will lead you what to say!"

So Sherri said, "All right, I'm going to do it!" And she put the coat across her arm and got out of the truck.

I told her Johnny Raye and I would wait in the truck.

This is what happened when Sherri got up to the door. Sherri walked slowly up the sidewalk and opened the gate and went on up to the door. She stood for a few minutes and looked at the shopping cart by the door.

I could see her smile, and then she knocked on the door.

Finally after awhile, we could see someone open the door just a crack, and then you could see someone peeking out.

Then the door just flew wide open, like she was expecting Sherri, and there stood this beautiful, beautiful, tiny, wee, small, bony, little old lady. She had the sweetest face and the most beautiful, pure snow-white-colored hair.

And Sherri looked at her and told the little old lady, "I know you're not going to understand this, but God has put you in my mind for the last few weeks. No matter whether I was awake or asleep I have seen you, and the Lord told me I was to find you and give you this coat because you have been very, very cold. So I give you this coat, in our dear Savior's name."

And that sweet, little, old Lady told Sherri, "Thank the Lord! Thank the Lord! Because I've needed a coat! But I don't have any money to buy one! And I have been really cold—so cold. Thank you and thank the Lord!"

And with these words, that beautiful, little old lady stuck her left arm straight out in front of her so that Sherri could help put that coat on her.

Sherri and that lovely, little old lady were hugging each other and smiling at each other.

That coat fit that little old lady, just as if it was made for her. She looked so beautiful in that light green coat. Bless her heart! They both kept smiling and hugging each other. In the truck, I was jumping up and down for joy and laughing and crying all at the same time.

All I could say was, "Thank you, Lord, thank you!" and "Johnny Raye, your mom has found her miracle lady. How wonderful God is, praise the Lord! Don't ever forget Johnny Raye, what God has done this day. Because your Mom and I didn't do anything. The Lord caused this miracle to happen. God is so good, so good! We only went where the Lord lead us to go."

And Johnny Raye looked at me, then at his mom, and the Miracle Lady and he patted my arm and said, "I know, Aunt Beth, but don't cry!"

I told Johnny Raye, "But, honey, you are so young, but not too young that you can't understand the billion-to-one odds of finding that little old lady. We could not have ever found her if God hadn't been leading us every step of the way. Just remember all your life, Johnny Raye, how good God is. Don't ever forget."

Johnny Raye patted my arm again and said, "I won't, Aunt Beth, but don't cry." And all he could do, bless his little heart, was to keep on staring at his mom and the miracle lady. Sherri didn't remember much after this and she and the miracle lady walked toward the truck, arm in arm. I wrote down the address, and we waved at that beautiful, little, old lady and yelled, "God bless you and Merry Christmas," to her as we drove off.

And don't ask me how in the world we got home, because I don't know. I know I was behind the wheel of the truck, but I truly do not remember driving home, not at all!

God had to be not my copilot but the pilot of that truck that afternoon. Praise God, praise God! Because we were laughing and crying all at the same time, plus we were praising the Lord too! But thanks to the Lord, He saw that we got safely home. When we got home, we told everyone what had happened, and at first they couldn't believe what had just taken place. But the facts were there so they finally did believe. Isn't God wonderful?

And all we did was trust, believe, and have faith in the Lord. A few days later, I told Nadine how the Lord led us to find, Sherri's "miracle lady" and Nadein started to cry, and she said, "I want that little old lady to have all of my mother's clothes!"

Wasn't that sweet of Nadine? I know Nadine's mother is looking down from heaven right now, and she is happy with the choice that Nadine has made in giving her clothes to Sherri's miracle lady. So Nadine and I went through the clothes, as they had been in that closet for ten years. We cleaned and packed everything in boxes. We took a small bag of groceries to the "miracle lady." (Sherri and I), and this is when we found out that her name is Eula and that she has a twin sister who lives with her and her sister's name is Beaulah.

They are so sweet, and we had a very lovely visit. And they did have lots of cats. Bless their hearts, not much of anything else though. We asked them to come and be our Christmas guests for our Christmas dinner, but they had made other plans. They thanked us anyway though. We asked if they would be offended if we brought them food after we had eaten our Christmas dinner. And they assured us that they would love that. We told them we would be bringing them the clothes too.

All the time we were there visiting with them, Sherri kept holding dear little Eula's tiny, bony, cold hand.

Sherri tried to explain to her how we had found her.

I'm not sure if they fully understood, but it was all right. They knew we loved the Lord, and that we loved them, so that's all that matters.

*   *   *   *   *

So come Christmas day, we had our dinner, and it was indeed the most beautiful Christmas that I had ever had. I feel God certainly did show us the true meaning of Christmas. We did not buy any Christmas presents or even send any Christmas cards, and it was truly a beautiful Christmas. After we had eaten, Sherri and I took food to our ladies on Kentucky Street. I fell in love with Beaulah. She is so sweet, while Sherri dearly loves her Eula.

We told Beaulah that we would see them in a couple of days with the clothes. Eula was off eating her Christmas dinner, and when she came home, Beaulah said she would go and eat. They were afraid to go off and leave their little house because they said someone would come and steal what little things they owned. It is so sad that we all have to be afraid all the time in our society. Praise God, there will come a time when the Lord will reign, and we won't ever have to be afraid of anything, never, never again.

The afternoon of the day we were going to take the clothes to our ladies, Sherri, Johnny Raye, and I were in the grocery store, and all of a sudden, Sherri started crying. I asked her what was wrong.

She said, "When we take the clothes to our ladies, we are not to go back, anymore. I guess our mission is finished."

I told her, "Bless your heart, Sherri. I know the Lord spoke to my heart yesterday but I didn't want to hurt you, so I didn't say anything. But you know, Sherri, we have to go forward to the next thing that the Lord wants us to do. So don't be sad, okay? The Lord loves our ladies, so don't worry about them."

And I hugged her and knew she would be all right. When we took the clothes that night, Eula wasn't there again so it wasn't as sad for Sherri as it would have been if Eula had been there. So we left the clothes, and we told Beaulah to tell Eula that we loved her also. We couldn't tell her we wouldn't be back anymore, because we didn't want to hurt them. So we hugged Beaulah and told her how much we loved them both. Bless their hearts, they are so sweet.

The good Lord has put so many people across my path that I feel that I am to pray for, and I feel very thankful and humble that God asks this of me. I did not understand at first, and I thought maybe Bob and I were supposed to change churches or go into the prison ministries or work for the rescue mission down off Baker Street. But after much soul searching and prayer, the Lord made me realize that I was going to be used in many places and many ways. I felt such a peace of mind after I learned of some of the ways the Lord was going to use me. I love it, I just love it. I have been searching all my life, wondering what purpose my life had. And now the Lord is using me. I sometimes write to perfect strangers; that beautiful small still voice tells me who to write to.

And the Lord uses my hand to write whatever that certain person needs to hear or sometimes I'm to simply share what the Lord has done in my life. And here is a lady that has always hated to write a letter, but the most important factor is the fact that I have had arthritis in my hands for a long time. The last two years it was so bad that it really was impossible for me to write or even to hardly use my hands. It was a daily chore to do things with my hands.

But you see when the Lord takes over and gains victory of you and you turn your body, soul, and heart over to Jesus, then you don't have to worry about anything any longer.

So when I sit down to write a letter or whatever I am to write, I just pray, and ask the Lord to bless the person whom I am to write to, for the glory of God.

And when I finish praying, each time my hand starts writing and my hand literally flies over the paper until I am done.

When I finish, I do read over what I've written because at the time I write, I do not know exactly what I have written, so I check for punctuation and spelling, and then I seal the letter in an envelope! Then I once again pray and ask the Lord to bless the letter as it goes on its way. Sometimes, I only have a name and a name of a town. So I just call the post office and ask for the zip code, and then I simply trust the Lord to send the letter where it's supposed to go.

All the letters, with the exception of *Mel Tari's* letter, have always gotten to where it's supposed to go.

But *Mel Tari's* letter is another story, and I will tell that "miracle" later in this book. Praise God! It is so simple, people only have to believe. And the Lord will move in marvelous ways in your life. And I believe, I believe.

I also share my gospel music tapes that we own. The Lord tells me who to share the music tapes with. And you know what? The Lord is so good. I've learned to let the Lord choose what songs people need to hear. Because it never fails whenever someone listens to their music tape or record they receive from God, whatever it is that the Lord wants them to receive. I've been told time and time again how a certain song or songs touched their hearts. So I love to share my love of God's music with God' d people. I do this for my dear Lord Jesus. It is so much fun! And now, because of Jesus and who He is, I am able to go up to complete strangers and speak to them about Jesus. Not because of anything that I can do or say but simply because of the goodness and mercy of our dear Jesus. Before Jesus came into my heart, I could not talk to a stranger or anyone else hardly unless they were family. I just was not an outgoing person at all. And it seemed as if I was always afraid of something, but thank the Lord, He took all of that fear away from me.

I could never in a million years ever, ever thank the Lord enough. Did you know how crippling fear can be? It destroys people's lives. We must not succumb to fear.

A few years ago, after I almost died, just because of a tooth problem, I developed the most deep-rooted fear of dying, and even of going to the dentist. It was so bad, the dentist did not even want to work on me anymore at all. And I do humbly, here and now, thank my Lord for taking that fear away and replacing it with His love and peace in my soul.

Then around this time, I had another one of my beautiful dreams. I seem to have dreams of the Lord quite frequently.

In this dream, I stood before this huge, most beautiful door that it is hard to even describe the beauty of the door.

It was the most beautiful door I've ever seen. And I stood before this door, and I felt very happy, even though I did not know why! And I knocked on the door, and as I could not see a doorknob, I waited. Then I knocked again, and suddenly the door opened. And there stood Jesus. It was so wonderful and such a beautiful feeling to look upon His face. All I could do was stand and look and stare at His beautiful, beautiful, face. How it shined and glowed, with a light and beauty not of this Earth.

And when He smiled, such joy filled my very being, I just can't describe that feeling, I just cannot! It was so precious, and so very exquisite.

And these are the words the Lord spoke to me, "Well, Beth, It's about time, It took you long enough to finally get here. Come on in, you have lots of work to do. So come in, and we will talk, about what needs to be done."

And I remember smiling back at Jesus and going through that door! I even can see that door shutting, but I do not remember what we talked about. I only know our conversation is deep, deep in my heart, whether I can remember it or not. I just know it's there. Yet I can see that big, beautiful door shutting. And ever since that dream, every single day, I am busy. I pray for the Lord to use me as His vessel. I want to do all that I can for my Lord Jesus Christ. It is a great privilege and honor and a wonderful joy to work for the Lord.

And it is so much fun and I feel so blessed because God is so wonderful, so wonderful. During this time I had been reading an article every week in a little neighborhood newspaper, written by Pastor James E. Phillips.

I really enjoyed the articles, and one afternoon the Lord spoke to my heart that I was to go to Pastor Phillip's church on the next Sunday morning. I prayed and prayed and I could not understand why God wanted me to go to a strange church. But each time that I prayed, I received the same answer, "Go!" So a few days before that Sunday, I was with my friend Nadine and I asked her if she wanted to go for a short ride. I tried to explain to her how the Lord wanted me to go to Pastor Phillip's church.

She did not understand why I was going to his church without knowing why I was even going. I told her, "Nadine, bless your heart, whatever the Lord wants me to do, I am willing, and it is not necessary that I understand."

But she is one of those persons that must have an explanation and a reason for everything. And I am beginning to see that there are a lot of persons, out in the world, just like that. Anyway, we drove around looking and we found the church, and boy, did I feel excited. My husband, Bob, later asked me where the church was, and when I told him, bless his heart, he got all upset because it isn't in a very good section of town. I told him once again how when God is with you, you have nothing to fear.

So that Sunday morning came, and as I was getting dressed, I prayed, "Lord I do not know why you want me to go to Pastor James E. Phillip's church. But you know I feel a little nervous, not because of where the church is but simply because these are strangers. So please go with me, Lord, and be with me."

I drove over to that side of town and pulled up in front of the church. And I said, "Lord, I don't understand at all why you want me here, but here I am!" Then I got out of the truck and walked into the church, slowly.

As I opened the big wide door, I could hear this beautiful male voice singing. I believe it was, "How Great thou Art!" I stood and listened and whispered, "Thank you, Lord, for bringing me here, for whatever purpose you have in mind, it's all right with me now. Here am I!"

There sitting behind the pulpit, on a chair was Pastor James E. Phillips, his beautiful, beautiful black face lost in singing to our Lord. Then all of a sudden, he saw me. He asked me if I was who he hoped I was. I smiled and told him, "Bless your heart, Pastor Phillips, I am Beth." He told me later that he just knew who I was.

You see I forgot to tell you, I had written to Pastor Phillips once and sent him and his family a gospel tape. He welcomed me to the church and made me feel so welcome! He explained that he was just starting out in this church. I explained to him how the Lord had told me to come to his church.

I said, "I still do not know why, but it is not necessary that I understand. I just want to serve the Lord." And since there wasn't anyone else there yet, I told him about the miracle lady.

And we talked for a while, and then I started to wonder if anyone else was coming. Then a beautiful, black lady came into the church, and Pastor Phillips introduced her to me as his beloved mother. She gave me a big hug, and bless her heart, she certainly made me feel mighty welcome, too. Then Pastor Phillips explained, again, how he was starting all over in this church and how his lovely, wife was the Sunday school teacher at their old church and how she was waiting for that church to find a replacement for her. So then she would be able to join her husband at his church.

Finally, Pastor Phillips said, "This is odd, usually, there are more people here, but since there aren't, we will proceed with the service."

So, Praise God, that wonderful and glorious service proceeded with just the three of us. We sang songs and then Pastor Phillips gave the morning message. And I was thrilled and took in God's word. As the Pastor drew to a close, he asked if I would like to give a testimony, and so praise God! I once again told the story of "the miracle lady."

Then Pastor Phillips told me, "I am being led by the Holy Spirit. May I come down where you are sitting?"

I nodded that it would be fine with me. And Pastor Phillips read from the Bible about receiving "the Holy Spirit." Then he asked me if I was scared.

And I told him, "When God is with me, I have nothing to fear, but yes I am a little bit nervous."

Then he asked me if I wanted to receive the Holy Spirit. And I could not say anything at first, and then finally I blurted out a very weak yes. You see I had heard lots of people speaking in tongues, but I thought, *That isn't for me.*

It's okay if they want to speak in tongues, but I don't want to. But praise God, the Lord had decided, I was ready. I could feel God's heavenly sweet spirit there with the three of us that day. How beautiful and sweet it was.

So Pastor Phillips told me, "Do not be afraid." And he asked me to stand so that he and his mother can simply pray for me and let

God do the rest. So I stood there rather stiffly, and they prayed for the Holy Spirit to have His way.

He asked me to repeat these words, "Holy Spirit, come into my life." And he kept telling me, "Relax and breathe deeply, take deep breaths, receive the gift of the Holy Spirit that God wants you to receive."

I kept standing there, not relaxing, but all of a sudden, Pastor Phillips told me, "Open your mouth, let the Holy Spirit pour out." And I felt his hand on my forehead, and then a fierce/burning, warm feeling came rushing over me.

It started from the top of my head, and I could feel it slowly, slowly, slowly flowing through my whole body. And the most glorious and wonderful feeling went all through me; my heart felt so happy. I felt happier than I have ever felt in my whole life. I wanted to shout with joy, and out of my mouth came these strange sounds. I could feel as if I was going upward in my spirit, and I felt like the Lord's and my heart touched briefly and soared and soared together. How beautiful was that moment! And as I opened my eyes, Pastor Phillips and his dear sweet Mother were both smiling.

And Pastor Phillips told me, "You have truly received the Holy Spirit!"

And they both hugged me and said, "May God keep continuing to bless you!"

I tell you that was so wonderful; that mere, simple words cannot describe the beauty. They invited me to come back to worship in their church anytime. When I left that church, I felt as if I was floating on one of God's beautiful clouds. And all I could do all the way home was say, "Praise the Lord" and "Thank you for your beautiful gift of your Holy Spirit!" And I was so excited, and later that afternoon, we went over to Sherri's apartment. And she took one look at me and wanted to know what had taken place with me, because she kept saying, "Your eyes, your eyes, they are so shiny and glowing! What has happened to you?"

After I told her, she kept saying, "Praise the Lord!"

I still don't understand why the Lord chose this man Pastor James E. Phillips to pray for me to receive His Holy Spirit. But it seems as if everything I am to receive and learn from God fills me with such joy. To have a teacher like Jesus is very, very glorious. And I've also learned that I don't even care about understanding why God wants me to do something.

I just do it, no questions asked. Then came the period in our life when the Lord decided we were going to move into this tiny, little house that we are in now. It was sure funny because we weren't even looking for a place to move to, because we didn't think we had enough money saved up. But one evening, Sherri, Bob, and I went over to visit their cousin Louise who lives in Oildale. Sherri was looking for a place to move into, and Louise told her of a little place down the alley from her. We went over and looked at the outside of the house, and when we came back to Louise's house, Sherri called the man who owned the house. He told Sherri the house rented for $350 a month, with a $200 deposit. That price was too much for Sherri, so she thanked him and hung up.

The Lord immediately spoke to my heart, "Wouldn't that be cheap if you only had to pay $350.00 a month for a house?"

And I thought, *Praise the Lord, I will call, because Lord you are so right, what a blessing that would be to pay only $350 a month.*

You see we had been paying over $625 a month for the last three to four years. So I called that man right back that owned that house. He told me we could come and look at it the next day, but he warned me that it wasn't in very good shape.

And he said it would be about thirty days before it would be fit to live in! So we went home, and Bob and I prayed that night. The next afternoon, we went over to look at the house.

And it was indeed a mess!

When we first walked in, Bob said, "No, no way will I live here!"

And I told him, "Bob, didn't we agree to let God lead us where He wanted us to go? If it is fixed up, it won't be so bad."

So we looked around, and the landlord told us he would put in some used carpet in the living room and in both bedrooms. Then we asked him, if we could use the deposit to buy the tile for the kitchen, the dining room, and the bathroom. And we told him we would put the tile down ourselves. And we wanted to put wallpaper in the kitchen and bathroom. And we would do a little bit of extra painting.

So he said, "Sure that's fine with me." Then he told us that we could do anything we wanted to with the house. Praise the Lord, all because God had went before us and prepared the way. So that entire month, Bob and I worked hard painting, putting the tile down, hanging wallpaper, and doing odds and ends that needed to be done. The landlord put the carpet in, and I prayed and asked God to bless the house. And lo and behold, the house started looking alive! And we brought our plants, and we did major work in the little yard. Then came the time for moving, and our newly found friends Jorine and Art Rogers insisted they wanted to help us move. And bless their hearts, they indeed did help us move. We moved and worked hard all day. Then as we finally moved the last load of furniture, we were here in our little, tiny, rented house, all four of us sitting down, resting.

Boy oh boy, were we tired! And we knew that we still needed to go to pay the rent. You see, that beautiful, tall landlord had given us the keys to this house the first time that we had met him, and we had never even passed any money between our hands or filled out any papers. When all of a sudden, here came the landlord and even with everything, stacked from the floor to the ceiling, he was pleased with how the house looked. He told us how he had grown up in this house, and he said it had been a long time since anyone had taken real good care of it.

And praise the Lord, the landlord even lowered the rent down to $325. Now isn't God wonderful? So that is how God moved us, and this is a small house, and little things are still wrong with it, like we actually went all winter without a heater. The heater was faulty and the landlord was going to get it fixed, but it is not fixed yet. But Bob and I felt there was a good reason for the heater not to be fixed—so that we could truly continue to feel compassion for the homeless by being cold as they were. So we never pushed the issue of the heater being fixed because we knew in our hearts that the Lord wanted us to learn how it felt to be really cold. God is so full of mercy and grace. We went from a big three-bedroom house with lots of junk, and the Lord sent along people that needed things so we gave a lot of extra things that we really didn't need away to people that did need them.

And we still have some things stacked in the spare bedroom. And eventually, Becky, our beautiful daughter, will come and get her things. But she moved into a trailer with her friend's family only about two miles from us. And that is a blessing in itself because she is so near. And our son Mike lives across town with his Karrie, and they are expecting a baby next month, in August. So finally, Bob and I are going to become grandparents for the first time. Praise the Lord! We can hardly wait, and I don't know who is more excited, Mike and Karrie or Bob and I. And Julie, who used to live with us too, she is out on her own. So even though this is a small house, we aren't home very often, it seems like, so it's okay. And boy oh boy, can you feel God's presence in our house. We may be only renting now, but it is such a blessing, because now we can do more for the Lord. Before, we were barely getting by with nothing left by the middle of the week. At last now, we can help God's people when we see someone who needs help.

After we got settled in, I remember seeing this movie where there were lots of soldiers on television. And I thought, as I watched that movie, how I did not think I was strong enough to be able to use a gun or a rifle, because the simple truth is I could not shoot anyone. And yet, that night, I had this beautiful dream. And as I said before, I believe God speaks to us in dreams. In this dream, I was standing back like a spectator, and I was watching all these soldiers with guns and rifles; it seemed just like a movie unfolding.

As I was watching all of those soldiers, my heart was crying. "Lord, please, I do not want to have to use rifles or guns or any sort of weapons like that. Lord You know my heart. Help me Lord, to be able to fight for You but not with guns or rifles."

And I could feel the people dying out in the world, even though in my dream I did not see dead people. And as I stood there watching those soldiers with their guns and rifles, a lovely woman came and stood by my side.

And these are the words that she spoke to me. "Beth, your weapon will not be a gun or a rifle. Your weapon will be the Word of God." Then she handed me a beautiful, beautiful Bible; the Bible glowed, especially the words, "The Holy Bible." They really glowed; it was such a special, beautiful Bible.

I took it gently in my hands and thanked her, and I whispered, "Thank you dear Lord Jesus!" And I turned to ask her another question, but she was fading away slowly, smiling all the while.

Then I could feel myself marching alongside those soldiers until we came to a town with hills on both sides of the road. It was such an odd town. As we all marched right down the middle of the road, a man came running out of a house yelling that he was going to kill us.

I started telling all the soldiers to run upon the side of the hills and said, "God will be your rock and your shield! God will protect you!" So all of us were going up the embankment, and the man kept yelling that he was going to shoot us.

Then he pulled a gun out, and I told him that Jesus loved him.

He shouted, "No!" and shot at us as we all yelled, "Jesus!"

And when the man shot the gun, a flag came out of the barrel, and it had the word "Jesus" on it. Then we all hugged the man, and he joined us on our journey.

All of a sudden, it seemed like we were going down a long hallway. And I kept seeing little children, and I thought, *How sweet they are. Jesus loves them so!* And I kept going up to each child and kept hugging them and telling them that Jesus loved them. And they followed us until we came to a door; then all of a sudden, the soldiers were all gone, and all the little dear children and I were standing at the door.

And I smiled and told them, "Do not be afraid, little ones, your Heavenly Father is waiting for you on the other side of this door. See, this is His Word. Stand on His Word, and all will be well."

And I showed them my beautiful, glowing Bible. Then I knocked on the door and it opened, and there stood our dear Savior, with His arms outstretched and smiling. And the dear little ones went through the door, all except one small, crippled child and he just stood there with tears streaming down his sweet little face.

He said to me, "I am not worthy to go there." And he pointed to where Jesus and all the children now stood together on the other side of the door.

I smiled and told him, "Yes, my child, Jesus loves you, and He wants you to come home now."

And the small crippled boy came toward me and put his little arms around my neck, and he whispered in my ear, "I want to go now. Please, I want to go home now."

Then I picked him up and carried that small, crippled boy through the doorway, and Jesus took him from me into His arms. Then Jesus motioned for me to go back through the door as I had much work left to do on Earth.

So with a brief glance backward, I strode back through the door with my Bible. As I got to the other side, I looked back through the door, and Jesus and all those children were smiling and waving at me. But best of all, as I gazed at them, I could see that little, crippled boy, he was standing beside Jesus, and Jesus was holding the little boy's hand.

And praise God, that little boy was not crippled anymore. His little legs were firm and straight. And I actually remember smiling in my dreams and shouting, "Thank you, Jesus, thank you, Jesus!"

And I woke up with those words of Praise for the Lord on my lips. You see, I feel so strongly that these dreams are so special and from our Heavenly Father.

Because about nine months ago, the Lord spoke to me and told me to make sure that I wrote down everything that He did in my life and to make sure it was exactly what He said and how the event happened. I have never forgotten that, so I write the things the Lord tells me to write. So all my writings are simply for the glory of my dear Savior. During the next few weeks, I was to learn more about the plan the Lord has for my life. I have prayed and prayed for the Lord to use me as His vessel. I am so thirsty for His word.

And the Lord told me I was to go to this church. So today, God sent me to a Quaker church here in Bakersfield.

Oh, how beautiful their people are! The Lord taught me so much today; the main thing is that it is all right to be quiet in our praise of the Lord. These people, these Quakers, were so blessedly peaceful. And my soul felt at peace, as I allowed their dear sweet, quiet souls to touch mine.

While we worshipped together, our hearts were all joined together in our love for God. That is what's important, not what color you have, what church you go to, or even what walk of life you come from because we are all one to God. He loves each one of us the same, no matter who we are. I found a peace and a beautiful quiet joy at their church. And I was welcomed into their midst. I gave them their message; they even seemed to know that they were to receive a message from God. Praise God, the Lord is so precious and wonderful! The people were not surprised at all that God was giving them a message. Maybe others in our world could take a lesson from these beautiful people of God on how to receive God's word without being surprised.

I can only praise the Lord for allowing me to be a vessel for His work. I humbly do thank God.

So now I come to the miracle of how I read the most beautiful book by Mel Tari (and how I finally, after a long time, got his address). One day, I went to my favorite used-book store, and I found a book called *The Gentle Breeze of Jesus* by Mel Tari. When I read the first page after I got home, I could not stop reading. What an extraordinary man—he writes so exquisitely beautiful. His writing makes your heart smile all the while that you are reading his book. And it makes you feel so excited about our Lord.

It is hard this time to really write of my feelings that I felt while I was reading his book. But I will try.

It was like meeting the twin person to my heart. His writing was exactly like I feel in my heart.

And it was the most beautiful experience, reading all the wonderful things that God had done on his island of Timor and to know that God is continuing to do all these miracles now today. As I finished reading the book, all at one sitting, I could not put it down.

The Lord spoke to my heart and told me that I was to write to Mel Tari and share some of my experiences with him. I looked at the inside of the cover of the book and saw that it was quite an old book, so I told the Lord, "Okay I will write to him, Lord, but you know I need an address. So please provide it to me, somehow, someway, when you are ready for me to write."

And I went on knowing that when the time was right, the Lord would help me get Mel Tari's address. Time went by and I shared with several friends how the Lord was going to help me get Mel Tari's address when it was time. After about a month, which during I prayed from time to time for the Lord to please not forget about Mel Tari's address, I came home from Bible study one Wednesday evening, and as I walked inside our house, the Lord told me to turn on the television station to the Christian station, TBN, and to get a piece of paper and a pencil and sit down and wait. Boy, did I get excited. I did not know what I was waiting for, but when the Lord speaks, I obey.

So I got the paper and pencil and sat down in front of the television with the TBN station on. I watched and waited.

After about one hour, I asked the Lord, "What am I waiting for, Lord?"

And all of a sudden, Paul Crouch started talking about their many missions. And they mentioned that Mel Tari was the head of their Indonesian missions, and let me tell you, boy oh boy, did my ears ever perk up.

And I said, "Praise the Lord, You are going to give me, Mel Tari's address, Lord, aren't you?"

Then Paul Crouch did not mention anything else, so I decided I would write to TBN, in Santa Ana, California, and ask them for Mel Tari's address.

Well, I sent them a few dollars and also asked them for Mel Tari's address. A few weeks later, about three weeks I think, I received a letter from TBN; they thanked me for the money, but bless their hearts, they never mentioned Mel Tari.

So I prayed and prayed, and I asked the Lord, "Lord, you never said things were going to be easy, and that's all right but you want me to write to Mel Tari, Lord. So please, give me his address, Lord, won't you, please? Tomorrow, I am going to call the station again, so please help me, Lord, I am believing in you,"

The next day, I called TBN and told three or four different persons the story of how the Lord wanted me to write to Mel Tari and that I needed his address, so would they please help me?

And finally, one lady gave me an address of Mel Tari. Was I ever excited, and that night, I sat down at our kitchen table (that is where I do all my writing) and I prayed for the Lord to bless me as I wrote to Mel Tari. Because you see, it is not by my might or anything I could possibly do that I write, it is by the power of God and because of who He is. Thank you, God for being there.

And praise the sweet Holy Name of Jesus, that letter was finally written to Mel Tari, and I mailed it off the next morning, asking God to bless that letter. Then I sat back waiting for a reply. But finally after one whole month, one day, I went to our mailbox, and there was Mel Tari's letter, returned to me saying no forwarding address was on file any longer. So I asked the Lord, "What should I do now, Lord, I am not going to give up."

And I picked the phone up and dialed the telephone number for the TBN television station. I explained to them what had happened and that they had given me an address for Mel Tari and how I had written to him and here a whole month later, the letter had come back. At first, this one lady kept telling me that there was nothing she could do.

But I tried to explain to her how the Lord did not have me do all that writing for nothing. And I told her, "I was not going to give up, because if the Lord wanted me to write to Mel Tari, then I was just not going to give up. I would be patient and wait, and the Lord would get me, Mel Tari's address." So she had me tell my story to a couple more ladies, until finally, one lady gave me a phone number for Mel Tari.

I thanked her and hung up. I immediately called that phone number, and praise the Lord, Mel had an answering machine, and I got to hear his dear, sweet voice telling me, "That he was out of the country, and to please leave my name, a short message, and a telephone number! And he would get back to me as soon as possible."

I was so excited. I left a short message, my name, and phone number; and again, I waited on my Lord. I just knew that when it was time, God would have Mel Tari call me.

And Bless the Holy Name of Jesus! About a week and a half later, exactly on the day of my birthday, Mel Tari did indeed call me.

Wasn't God good? All of that time trying to get Mel Tari's address, but it was to take all that time, so that Jesus, could have Mel Tari call me exactly on that day, for my Birthday. God is so infinitely wise.

When I heard Mel Tari's voice, I said, "Praise God, the Lord had you call me on my birthday. What a beautiful birthday present that the Lord has given me!"

And Mel Tari asked me if it was really my birthday? I assured him it was. And bless his heart, Mel Tari sang "Happy Birthday" to me. How unbelievably sweet that moment was. It felt truly, truly like Jesus was singing "Happy Birthday" to me. And he gave me his address and we talked some.

After I hung up, Bob asked me, "Who in the world was that on the phone to make your face glow like that?"

I was so overwhelmed, I blurted out, "That was Mel Tari, praise the Lord. God is so good! And Mel Tari even sang "Happy Birthday" to me! All that time trying to get Mel Tari's address was all worth it because the Lord had him call especially today. Isn't God wonderful?"

Bob looked at me and said quietly, "Well, I certainly will never be able to top that birthday present."

I laughed and hugged him and I gave him a big kiss as I told him, "Honey, this is not a contest, you do not have to top this birthday present or anything else. I love you! But this is the most exciting thing that has ever happened to me on my birthday."

And the rest of my birthday, forty-two years old at that, was wonderful too! So I finally sent that letter once again to Mel Tari. And during this time, I had ordered another book by Mel Tari, *Like A Mighty Wind*. It was every bit as inspiring as Mel's other book. Bless his heart, he writes about Jesus so simply and so utterly beautiful. It touches your heart and makes you want to know Jesus even more. I will ever be so grateful to the Lord for Mel Tari. I can't wait to read his new book.

At our church, we have a lovely couple that are great teachers. We always look forward to our Wednesday night Bible studies. Bill and Denise Davis are getting ready to go out on their own to minister to the Lord's people. They are so sweet and so full of God's love.

And praise the Lord, they get so excited about working for our Lord, too—just like me! And so we are so very fortunate at our church to have them as our teachers. They are waiting for God to take them exactly where He wants them to go.

One Wednesday night, at Bible study, Brother Bill shared with all of us during the class about a vision that he had a few nights earlier. And as he shared this beautiful vision, I felt a deep stirring in my heart, and I thought, *Lord, what a beautiful, beautiful story that would make such a beautiful song.* So I went home afterward, and these are the words for Brother Bill's vision that I put for a song. I wrote the words, but I do not have the tune yet.

Raindrops from Heaven

There was a man of God, whose name was Bill.
He only lived to do God's will!
He prayed to the Lord to receive a blessing.
He cupped his hands together and prayed that he was worthy.
Bill lifted his hands toward heaven and
prayed for his hands to be clean.
Dear Lord, he thought, my hands look so dirty.
But I am your man, and I will do my duty!
The Lord looked down on Bill, and He felt such an overwhelming
feeling of love for him that God let the tear drops fall from His eyes,
And he let them fall as raindrops.
They fell from heaven with joy for Bill.
And the raindrops, as they fell, were singing,
Hallelujah! Hallelujah! Hallelujah! Hallelujah!
And so those raindrops from heaven washed Bill's hands clean!
Bill continues to sing, "Thank you, Jesus! Thank you, Jesus, for the
glorious singing of the raindrops, as they fall from my Savior's eyes!
The Lord has redeemed me. He has set my soul free!
I will work all the days of my life for Thee!!"
So please, Dear Jesus, keep letting those raindrops fall
while they sing, Hallelujah! The raindrops are singing,
Hallelujah! Hallelujah! Hallelujah! Hallelujah!
Hear that glorious sound? As the raindrops sing,
"Hallelujah! Hallelujah! Hallelujah!"

Praise the Lord, can't you just hear that exquisite singing? Bill described to all of us that the sound was like a chorus of Heavenly Angels, like clear crystal love coming down from our Lord. I found these beautiful words one day, and I felt like the words spoke how I wanted to live my life:

> My heaven is to please God and glorify Him and to give all to Him and to be wholly devoted to His glory. All my desire is to glorify God. I see nothing else in the world that can yield any satisfaction besides living for God, pleasing Him and doing His whole will.

I believe if each and every one of us would do our share of what the Lord wants done, there would not be any lost souls out there in the world.

There is another story of how the Lord works in such wondrous ways. One day, I was reading of a lady that was in a nursing home here in our town of Bakersfield and how she could not talk from a previous injury. The Lord spoke right then and there that I was to take her a tape of gospel music and a bookmark from the Christian book store. I took these things with a brief note to this lady that Jesus did indeed love her and left them with the nurse in charge. The next day I shared with my sister-in-law, Sherri, the article in the newspaper about that lady and how she had touched my heart. In this story, the lady had an accident and was in a coma for a while; then she was transferred to many different hospitals. No one could ever find out who she was or where she came from. Her people had tried to find her but without success.

And finally since she could not talk and her hands were all drawn up from disuse, one brave, beautiful nurse's aide decided to try to find out who this lady was. During an activity at the hospital one afternoon, where some persons were singing, "Jesus Loves Me," this nurse watched as this lady, whom no one knew, silently mouthed the words to that song. And this nurse knew there was a person inside of her that was aware and not just a vegetable.

So they doubled their efforts to find out who she was. And a patient, in that nursing home, named Kelly, who by the way has the most beautiful red hair, suggested to the nurse a technique to use to help find out who this lady was!

And it did indeed work, and praise the Lord, they found out names and addresses of loved ones. So they finally were able to bring this lady and her loved ones together.

Anyway as I told Sherri this story, she told me, "I want to go and meet this lady." So we prayed if it was God's will that we would go visit this lady at the nursing home.

A few days later, Sherri, Kathleen (a dear friend of ours from church), and I all went to the nursing home. We met that lady, and then after we visited a few more rooms of sweet little souls, I told Sherri about that beautiful black man that was asleep with the Bible in front of him. And she told me she wanted to see him, so while Kathleen went visiting another room, Sherri and I went back to that man's room. And he awoke with the biggest, brightest, warmest smile on his face. And he welcomed us, and we told him that we were from Sunrise Church and that we were visiting people. Well, bless his heart, he told us who he was and then how God came into his life and how the Holy Spirit had entered his heart and soul. And he was praising God all the while. Then he told us how he used to be a rhythm and blues singer and how he was from Rison, Arkansas. Then Kathleen came in and stood with us as we listened with fascination to Jack. Then, and Praise God, this was so wonderful, Jack started to sing to us. Bless his beautiful soul! How he blessed us and how very beautiful he was. Lying in that bed, unable to move around much, we had come to make him feel good. Instead, he was making us smile, making our hearts and souls smile with joy.

I just ask the good Lord to bless Jack Allen. Those beautiful songs he sang—some he made up—they were songs so sweet, so pure, and so full of love for God that they made our hearts fill with such happiness to be able to hear Jack sing of his love for our Dear Savior.

It was just too precious for words! We promised him that we would come back to visit him and the rest of those dear souls in that nursing home.

Bless their hearts each and every one of them. Then just before we left, Jack spoke up and looked right at Sherri, and he told her, "It's not right to even kill a fly, Jesus says, it's not right to kill any of His creatures!"

And at this point, I must tell you, that during a time when Sherri was reading her Bible every day, she would ask a lot of questions, and one of her questions that she asked of everyone was, "Is it right to even kill a fly?"

And as Jack said those words, I thought, *Lord, how good you are, you are using Jack to answer Sherri's question, from about a year ago.* She had not found anyone who or could give her a satisfactory answer. And here after all this time, the Lord was letting Sherri know that He had not forgotten her and her question! Praise God, and I know some people may feel that it was a silly question; but you see, to Sherri, who has such a beautiful, warm, and kind heart and who loves all animals dearly, this was a real and important question. And I looked at Sherri and she looked at me, after Jack had said those words to her, and we both got the biggest grins on our faces. Because we knew, we knew, how wonderful God is, and all we could do was say, "Praise God, praise God!"

And then we told Jack goodbye and that we would see him again. And all three of us left that nursing home shouting, "Glory to God" and "Hallelujah!" We were so filled with God and so thankful because God was and is so good. We have went back, and we are blessed more each time we go. That is how good our Heavenly Father is, because we go to help elevate the loneliness for these dear persons in the nursing home, and instead we are all so very, very blessed. And each time, dear Jack Allen sings his beautiful songs to us. May God continue to heal and bless him. A few days later after we had visited Jack Allen in that nursing home, I was at home, and I saw a spider by the bathtub, and it had fallen in the tub as it filled up with hot water, and the poor thing was dead.

So I picked it gently out of the water and placed it on the side if the bathtub. (Don't ask me why I did that, because I truly don't know.) The next morning I decided to clean the bathroom, and I thought of that dead spider, but when I went into the bathroom, I went over to the bathtub, and there was that spider! But praise God, it was alive! Alive! And as I watched that spider, those words came back to me that Jack Allen had spoken, "It's not right to even kill a fly."

So I said, "Praise God, I guess you want that spider alive, Lord, but, if you don't mind, I'm going to put it outside." So I very gently picked that spider up and put it outside on the bathroom window sill.

And once again, I could hear those words being spoken, just as clear as a bell. "It's not right to even kill a fly."

And I smiled and said, "I hear you, Lord, I hear you."

Then a few hours later, I was getting ready to use the curling iron on my hair. And bless your hearts, I could not believe this happened to me! But I promised the Lord that I would tell you, anyway. So here is the rest of the story that happened to me that afternoon. Anyway, I was curling my hair, and out of the blue, I glanced down at the sink, and I saw this ugly, old roach crawl out of the drain. As I looked down and saw that roach, my first instinct was to smash it, which is what I have always done to spiders and roaches.

But as I stared at that roach, I once again could hear the voice of Jack Allen (or was it God?) telling me, "It's not right to kill even a fly."

And I groaned and said, "Lord I will obey, but I can't stand spiders or roaches! Can't they, please, stay outside?"

And I got inside the linen closet and pulled out a small towel, and I was going to pick the roach up gently and put it outside. And I got close to that roach, but as I stood there and was looking at it, I swear too you, it just simply disappeared, in thin air! It just disappeared! I stood there in amazement, in pure astonishment and asked, "Lord, where did it go? Where in the world did it go?"

And I pulled everything, the hamper, and trashcan away from the wall and looked and looked for that roach. I shook my head and rubbed my eyes, but there was no roach. And so I said, "I hear what you are saying, and I will not kill a spider or that roach, Lord. And how wonderful You are, Lord."

And for two days, the old devil kept telling me not to tell the story because it was stupid. And sadly to say, I did not tell the story, until one evening, a few nights later, I just blurted out to my sister-in-law, Sherri, the story of the roach and that spider. And she said, how beautiful that was, and didn't I see that I had been tested by God to see what I would do! I agreed that I believed that. But I thought I still won't tell anyone else. Then as Bob and I drove home that night, I could not help myself. I told Bob what had happened in our bathroom, about the spider and the roach. Bob just smiled and did not say much. Then after we were home, Bob was reading the Sunday funny papers, and all of a sudden Bob said, "Well, I can't believe this, no, it can't be. Listen to this, you know that story you told me on the way home?"

I told him, "Yes, I remember."

Bob said, "Listen to this; here is a cartoon."

It was a *Beetle Bailey* cartoon, and it showed two men looking down at the ground at some ants, and one of the men was saying, "I could just smash those stupid ants with one blow of my hands!"

And the other man was shouting, "Wait, wait, what is happening?"

Then the other man said, "Oh, you'd better not kill those ants, the sky is getting dark! I think you just made God very angry!"

And I started laughing and shouting, "Praise the Lord!"

You see God, put that cartoon in the paper to reaffirm my story that I told Bob! Isn't God good?

Bob said, "I just cannot believe the things that God does for you. This is incredible, but yes, I believe God is reaffirming your story."

A few weeks later, Bob and I came back from being out of town. And I called our daughter Becky to tell her that we were home again. But Becky's friend Stacy told us that Becky was feeling real sick and that Becky was in bed. So I told Stacy not to wake her up and just to tell Becky that we loved her, that we hoped she felt better by tomorrow, and that we would call Becky in the morning.

During the night, I had another one of my wonderful dreams. God is so good, so good. In my dream, Becky was lying in a bed and all over her chest, she had these horrible, horrible, horrible, growths. They were so ugly, I have never seen anything so awful-looking. They looked like a fungus of some sort. And in this dream, I was kneeling and praying for Becky because I knew that she was dying.

I prayed, "Dear Lord, she is your daughter first before she is mine; please, heal her and take those terrible growths off of her. Please make her whole again. In the sweet name of our dear Jesus, I beg of you to heal her, my Father."

Then I rose up and left that house. It was a strange house, nothing was familiar to me at all. Then I remember coming back into the house; I don't know where I had been, but there stood this older type-looking man in the middle of the room.

He was dressed just like us—He wore beige-tan-colored pants and a red and white plaid shirt. And He had the most beautiful, pure, snow-white hair and the most wonderful, wonderful-looking face! I could sense that He was old, but there were no wrinkles on His face at all. It is very hard to describe how glorious and how beautiful His face looked. I could only stand and stare, and then finally I asked Him, "Who are you?"

Then He told me His name softly, and I thought He said, "John."

But I wasn't sure, so I asked Him again. "Your name is John?"

He shook His head, "No," and He said loudly this time, "My name is God!"

I said, "Is that you, God? Praise the Lord, is it really you, God?"

He kept smiling at me and shaking His beautiful head and said. "Yes!"

Then He pointed into the other room, where we could both see Becky; she was still lying on that bed, and He softly told me, "Do not worry, my child, I have healed your daughter, Beckany, and she will be all right now."

I took His left hand and I said, "Thank you, God, thank you!"

I was so overwhelmed at that moment. And I rushed into the other room, and, as I stood looking down at Becky, I could see she was indeed all right. Those ugly growths were all gone—there was no sign of them ever being on her body. I glanced over my shoulder and shouted, "Thank you again, Lord"

And God was just standing there watching Becky and me. And He was smiling and nodding His dear sweet head at us. Then I came back into the other room, and stood looking into His wondrous, beautiful face, and He just kept smiling at me!!

That smile, there simply are no words to describe His smile. It was more glorious than anything you could ever hope to see. "Praise God, how good and merciful He is!"

Then the Lord turned to go toward the door, and I followed right directly behind Him. (I do not know where I thought I was going.)

I was only a few inches behind Him; I could have put my hand up and touched His back. I did not though; and when the Lord came to the door, I expected Him to reach down and turn the doorknob to go out through the door. But He just kept right on walking, and He walked right through that solid door! I tell you, that was a wondrous feeling—watching Him walk through that door (not stopping at all).

I put my hand up and touched the door in the middle and whispered, "Thank you, God, thank you!"

Then I reached down at that right-hand side of the door and turned the doorknob and opened the door. I saw nothing on the other side, but I put my head out and yelled, "Thank you, Lord, thank you. I love you."

Then all of a sudden, it was like I was in another room, and I could see it was like a courtroom. I did not see anyone I knew, but I could see a Judge sitting up front and lots of people in the background.

Then I saw three men, and one of them turned toward me, and I saw it was the Lord again, He still had on those same clothes that He had worn earlier—those same tan-beige pants and that red and white plaid shirt. He smiled at me and motioned for me to come closer, and I could hear myself saying, "Praise the Lord, there you are again, Lord! What are you doing this time? It's so good to see you again so soon"

Then the Lord motioned toward the other two men and I heard Him tell me, "Come and listen closely to what happens here in this court, so that you can be prepared to help defend the people who will need help soon. So listen closely to what is going to be said here."

And I was aware of words being said, but when I woke up, I could not remember any words.

But I believe the words are deep in my heart to use when the time comes that it will be necessary for me to do whatever the Lord intends for me to do for His people. Praise the Lord, anyway, isn't the Lord good?

As soon as I woke up the next morning, I called Becky to see how she was feeling. She told me, "It's strange, but I don't feel sick anymore, Mom."

And I shouted, "Praise the Lord, Becky, of course you aren't sick anymore, the Lord healed you last night!"

And He gave you a brand-new name, Becky; God called you Beckany. Isn't that a beautiful name? When you get to Heaven, your new name is going to be Beckany."

I told her about the dream, and Becky told me, "Mom, that is beautiful, and He must have healed me because I feel fine now."

Then two days later after that dream, Becky, Stacy, and I went to a baby shower. As they were getting ready to go home, Becky told me she would see her dad and me over the weekend.

I want to make this perfectly clear, we did not know that Becky was going out of town at all.

During that night, I had another dream, and in this dream a voice kept telling me over and over, "Becky is lost! Becky is lost!"

And I could hear myself telling this voice, "Becky, can't be lost. She is at home asleep." Then I added, "But, Lord, if this is you telling me she is lost, then, I'm sorry that I questioned you, and if she is truly lost or something is wrong with her, Lord, please, keep her safe." Then I could see a big, giant hand giving me a book, and it had these words on the book: Find the answer in God!

Then I woke up, and I had this overwhelming desire to get up and pray and read the Bible. Those words kept coming back to me, "Becky is lost!" And I tried to call Stacy's house, but no one answered. For the entire time the next day, which was Sunday, I could hear those words over and over again. So I continued to pray and I asked everybody I saw to pray. And yet, I knew that Becky was all right and that the Lord was taking care of her. Then around 4:00 p.m., Karrie, our daughter-in-law to be, called and asked us if we had seen Becky and Stacy. I told her no, but I told her about that dream that I had the night before.

People do not question me anymore when I tell them what the Lord says or is doing, because people have seen the mighty hand of God working in my life. So anyway, Karrie then said, "Becky and Stacy had borrowed Mike's car (Mike is our son) last night and they had went out of town. But they promised Mike that they would be home by 10:00 a.m., but here it is 4:00 p.m. and no one has heard anything from them. Mike is worried because that is not like Becky. She always comes back when she says she will."

I told Karrie, "Praise God, that dream did mean something! I'll call you and Mike after church tonight to see if they have gotten home! Let's pray for Becky and Stacy's safety though."

So around 10:00 p.m., after church, we talked again to Mike and Karrie, and we all agreed that we were worried. The girls still had not come home. I told Mike about that dream and how that voice kept saying, "Becky is lost!!" So we prayed once more. Then about an hour later, Stacy's mom called us and said that the girls had come home and that they were fine but really tired and that Becky promised to call me in the morning. The next day, Becky came over, and I took her shopping as we had not had a chance to buy her birthday present yet. I told her how worried we had all been. Then Becky looked at me and she told me, "Mom, don't get upset, but we were lost."

And I smiled and shouted, "Praise the Lord, Becky, God knew you were lost. And I got up and prayed for you."

Then I told her about the dream and the voice and how it kept telling me, "Becky is lost!"

And Becky said, "Well, Mom, the Lord was watching over me because we weren't only lost once but three different times. Not for very long, but still, we were indeed lost."

As I listened to Becky talking to me, I could hear that voice once again in my mind, telling me, "Becky is lost!" But praise the Lord, God was watching over Becky and Stacy.

You see, Becky had been trying to get closer to the Lord. A few weeks before all of this, Becky had called in the middle of the night. And she was hysterical and I asked her what was wrong.

And this is what Becky told me, "Mom, Satan is trying to come against me; he was making horrible noises, trying to speak to me, but I don't want to hear him, so I just kept on praying to God. But I am scared, Mom. Please, pray for me."

And I told her, "Honey, it's okay. Satan can't have you—you belong to God! I dedicated you and Mike to God a long time ago. You are a child of God's. Satan can't and does not have any power over you. We rebuke Satan away from you, in the name of Jesus Christ!"

And we prayed and then I told her I was going to call some friends to pray and that I would call her right back.

After I hung up, I got down on my knees and asked God to bless Becky and to help her. Then I asked God who I should call. And the Lord gave me the names, and I called people from our church and also my sister-in-law Sherri and our friend Ruth. I also called Don and Ellen in Dinuba, California, and quickly explained to them what had happened. Each one assured me that they would pray for Becky as soon as we hung up.

Then I called Becky back and she said, "Mom, I can feel all of your prayers. God is watching over me now. I am all right!"

So even though some people do not want to admit Satan is alive, he is. But praise our God, God is the King of us, and He's promised to be our rock and to protect us. So when we have God in our lives, we have nothing to fear. So we must all bury ourselves in God's Word. Study your Bible. Learn God's Word, and lean on His teaching.

Do not depend upon any man because we must set our sights on Jesus. Jesus died on the cross for our sins. So believe in Jesus. Jesus is coming back for us soon.

And the Door to Heaven Is Still Open, so Come on In!

A few weeks ago, friends of ours from church, Patty and Jim Spiller, asked me to make two gospel tapes because they wanted to give some friends of theirs some music to bless them because these friends of theirs needed their spirits lifted up. And the Lord can indeed speak to people through music! So I cheerfully made two tapes and took the tapes to church the following week, not thinking something was about to happen.

A few nights later, we were having an ice cream social at our church after our services, and Jim came up to me. This is what he said, "We want to thank you for those tapes, but I listened to them, and they aren't exactly all the same songs that you put on the tape that you gave us. And also as I played the tapes, one side (in fact the same side of each tape) played fine, but the other side of both of the tapes was all garbled and you could not understand the singing."

I looked at him and said, "Well, bless your heart, I don't understand that, but give me the tapes back and I will tape them again on each of the bad sides. And as far as the songs, Jim, I thought you understood about my taping. I am taping for the Lord. I do not choose the songs for whomever I am taping the songs for. I do not choose any of the songs. So, the Lord evidently did not want your friends to hear the same songs as you and Patty. And you see, I cannot tape your way because the Lord wants your friends to hear Him. So I must tape as the Lord leads me to do—not as man wishes but the way of the Lord."

"I will fix the tapes, so bring them next Wednesday night, and we will see if they play or not. I have a feeling that the Lord is fixing to do a miracle again."

Afterward I went outside of the church, and my sister-in-law Sherri was standing out in the coolness of the night. I explained to her what Jim had just told me, and she smiled saying, "Remember at Christmas time how that tape would not play for Bernice? You say he played those tapes for himself?"

I told her that yes he had.

"Well, don't you see? Those tapes were not meant for his ears. They are for his friends," Sherri said to me.

I smiled, and we both said, "Praise the Lord, that is what happened!"

So the next Wednesday night, after Bible study, Jim gave me the tapes. I took them and told him, "Bless your heart, I know these are going to play fine; you weren't meant to hear these tapes because they were for your friends. Don't ask me why because I do not understand how God works. But I will take them home and play them and we will see."

So Bob and I went home, and I asked Bob to sit and listen while I played each tape. We sat down and played one tape, and it played beautifully on both sides.

Then I played the other tape in our other cassette player in the other room, and praise God, it played fine on both sides too! So I sat down and wrote out the story of Sherri at Christmas time and how the tape she gave to Bernice would not play.

The next day, I took the tapes and the written account of Sherri and Bernice, and when I got to Jim and Patty's house, Jim answered the door, and I handed him the tapes and the note, and I smiled very broadly, I admit. I get so excited whenever God lets Jesus do something so wonderful as these small miracles.

Or is there any such thing as a small miracle? In my book, there are no small miracles. I told Jim, "Bless your heart, Jim, the tapes play beautifully! Both sides too. No problem with the sounds at all; isn't God fantastic?"

"Just give each friend a tape and do not try to figure out which tape for which friend. Trust in the Lord; He has it all planned out. We will see you and Patty at church next Sunday and tell Patty that we love her. God bless you, both!"

Then later that month, our church had a camp meeting. That was a whole week of hearing God's word; how utterly glorious that was—twice a day at that! The mornings we had Bible study, and then in the evenings we had more singing and a sermon from a guest speaker. Boy oh boy, did Jorine, Kathleen, and I enjoy listening to God's Word!

*　　*　　*　　*　　*

Kathleen has a son named Jerold. He was dropped on his head when he was an infant and has had severe brain damage ever since. He is thirty-two years old, and we have been praying for him, and praise the Lord, I can see when God touches him!

Jerold is like a child most of the time, but bless his heart, he speaks the most profound things sometimes.

And now he will shake your hand, and I do mean shake it, and his smile is so sweet. Bless his heart!

And one night at the camp meeting, the Lord spoke to my heart to go and take Jerold down to the front of the auditorium and to pray for him. Then the Lord told me to tell Jerold to go further on down to the front of the stage where his mother was praying. (I found out later the Lord had told Kathleen that she was not to be the one to take Jerold down to the altar.) Just before Jerold reached his mother's side, she looked up and saw him coming.

She opened her arms wide, and Jerold went straight into her arms. How beautiful that was! She loves her son so much.

Then she took Jerold to the front of the stage, and the ministers all gathered around him and prayed for him. Then a few minutes after the ministers had moved on to pray for another person, a man came up to Kathleen and introduced himself as a minister of God from a little town near Bakersfield, and he told her that he knew that he was a perfect stranger to her but that God had spoken to him that he was to tell Kathleen that her son was healed in the name of Jesus. (Praise God, Jerold was healed!) And he also told her God said, "Her son would be teaching the Word of God"

She was also told that she was to teach Jerold from God's Word, the *Holy* Bible. It was so moving and so wonderful; Kathleen was praising the Lord, and you could hear her all over that big auditorium. And Jerold, bless his heart, he just kept smiling.

Praise the Lord, praise the lord! God is so good!

Then the next day, I could hear the Lord telling me all day long these words, "Expect a miracle."

Well, I have truly seen the Lord move in such a mighty way that when the Lord says to expect a miracle, I expect. I walked around all day, waiting for what I did not know or care; I just knew God was going to do another miracle.

By late afternoon, nothing had happened, and it was time to go to the last camp meeting session. Just before we left, I saw the camera sitting on the table, and Bob looked so handsome, I wanted to take a picture of him.

He told me, "No, not until I take your picture first!"

So I told him okay. And he took my picture—we have an instant polaroid camera—and Bob took the picture out of the camera and handed it to me. I glanced at it and shouted, "Praise God, look Bob, look!"

Bob and I stood there watching as that picture developed right before our eyes. And right across my whole face and at the top above my head was a beautiful white, wispy-looking cloud. All the week before, I had prayed for the Lord to send His guardian angels to protect all of us. And there in that picture was my guardian angel. I mean there was no doubt in my heart or mind at all. We do have a personal guardian angel.

And I could hear the Lord speaking to my heart, in His beautiful, still, soft, silent voice telling me, "There, behold your miracle!"

Bob shook his head and told me, "That will go away."

I smiled and told him, "No, this is God's miracle; I believe that that is my guardian angel."

Then I took Bob's picture in exactly the same place. It turned out normal. Then I even took another picture of the same scene without anyone in the picture. It was normal too.

Then Bob and I looked at that picture again, and that beautiful, white, wispy cloudy form was still in the picture. Praise the Lord, it is still there, today, in that picture of me!

Isn't God wonderful? Not because of me or anything I said or did but because God is God! Praise His holy name!

I have had a horrible, horrible spiritual battle against Satan to write this book. No one will really truly ever know how bad it's been, and it doesn't matter anymore.

I thank the Lord for being with me all through the fight. We know we can count on Him—He is our shield.

Do you believe in miracles? Well thanks to our dear friend Jesus, I believe in miracles. Thank you, Lord! Miracles are real, and so is our Lord. He is no fairy-tale person; He is alive! Alive and well and He is living today!

I want God to shine His light so brightly through me that you will have absolutely no doubt. We are God's light in this world. There are so many persons out there in the world that do not know our Jesus.

So let's, each and every one of us, go out and tell them.

Let's tell them of a man who died on the cross for our sins so that we might have eternal life. Let's tell them that this man is Jesus and that He is the son of our living God. God can use each and every person. You may think you are not worthy or just that you have no special talent, but believe me, take it from a person who thought those ideas too, you are indeed a new creature when the Lord sends His Holy Spirit to touch you. I was a quiet woman who tried to be a good wife, a good mother, and a good person. I may have been these things, but now that God has come into my heart, I am a brand-new person, not by my might or anything I have done but because of God and who He is.

I can do things I never in a million years dreamed was possible. But simply because I believe and I trust and I have faith and mostly because I love God, I go forth with a heart full of fire that the Holy Spirit has put there.

I am so hungry for His Holy Word. No matter how much I read about Jesus and His dear Father, our Almighty God, I still thirst for more knowledge of them. Praise their Holy Names! But for the first time in my life, I am not searching blindly. When I did not even know what I was searching for, I would go outside, day or night, and look up in the sky and wonder what this thing called life is.

Then I started getting so bogged down by this world that I was depressed by everything that I saw or did.

And it seemed everyone I talked to or met were so negative about life. I honestly can't give an exact moment when I surrendered my life completely. But I do know it all goes back to that time when I almost died the last time and all over a simple tooth problem. Actually, I have almost died three different times, but the last time, I guess because of how bad the world seemed to be coming made me decide that I did not want to live my life the same way that I had been doing before. Once I made that decision, I have been so happy. And I just praise the Lord every minute of the day and night for what he has done for me. And I thank Him, and I vow to continue to work for the Lord until the day or night comes when He will come to take us home.

That doesn't mean life is all peaches and cream, but through the battles that I go through, I become stronger in my faith.

And I have learned that we can't live our lives as an island—we need other people in our lives. By praying and sharing with others, we grow stronger and we are able to cope better with life in general. We need to tear down Satan's strong holds. We need to fight against those rulers and authorities, against the powers of this dark world, and against the spiritual forces of evil. So stand up for good and stand up for God and His Kingdom. Stand up and help the homeless persons, the children, those that are hurting, and the dying souls out there.

Someone once said to me, "What's the use of trying to reach people? Besides, everyone knows about God and His Son, Jesus."

And that, my friends, made me cry in my heart. Because everyone doesn't know about Jesus. Oh, they may have heard of Him, but they do not have a personal relationship with Him. And that is we all need, a one-on-one relationship with our Lord. And as far as what's the use? If we give up, there will be no hope for all mankind. And I do not want to live like that. I want to see hope in everyone's face.

So as for me and my house, we will serve the Lord all the days of our lives. And so I leave you with these words that I have written as the good Lord has directed me.

May God have mercy on all of us. And finally, remember my brethren, be strong in the Lord and in the power of His might that He gives us to overcome our enemy. Put on the whole armor of God that He may be able to stand against the wiles of the devil.

> For we wrestle not against, flesh, and blood, but against spiritual wickedness in high places. Therefore, take unto you the whole Armor of God, that Ye may be able to withstand in the evil day, and having done all too stand, stand therefore, having your loins, girt about with Truth, and having the Breastplate of righteousness; and your feet shod with the preparation of the Gospel of Peace; Above all, taking the shield of Faith, where with, Ye shall be able to quench all the fiery darts of the wicked. And take the Helmet of Salvation, and the Sword of the Spirit, which is the Word of God! Peace be to the Brethren, and Love with Faith, from God, the father, and the Lord, Jesus Christ.
>
> Grace be with all them that Love our, Lord, Jesus Christ in sincerity. (Ephesians 6:10–24, KJV)

Don't wait too long; Jesus is calling you, today.

The door to heaven is still open, come on in, come home! Come home!

Amen.

Mankind: Read Ezekiel chapters 33 through to the end of Ezekiel.

He which testifieth these things saith, surely I come quickly. Amen
Even so, come, Lord Jesus.

—Revelation 22:20)

Permission received by these persons to use them in my book:

Bob Reeves
Becky Hardin
Mike Hardin
Sherri Frey and (son) Johnny Raye Hunter
Scott Frey
Don and Ellen Krause
Bernice Wilkerson
Robert Rossman
Pastor James E. Phillips
Mel Tari
Kathleen Hatfield and son
Jerold Bill and Denise Davis
Patty and Jim Spiller
Jack (Jackie) Allen
Nadine La Rose
Stacy Pryor
Jorine and Art Rogers
Jilie Weare

About the Author

Beth Reeves is now a widow who lives in Galena, Kansas. She is an ordinary lady with an extraordinary love for Jesus. She preaches, sings, and helps others. She and her late husband worked with the homeless. She loves all people. And she wants you to know if you're reading this book that Jesus loves you.

CPSIA information can be obtained
at www.ICGtesting.com
Printed in the USA
LVHW04s0523060718
582741LV00001B/21/P